PostMission

World Mission by a Postmodern Generation

D0325284

'Good design, varied content, this book will be really valuable for those considering mission work over the next few years.'
Gerard Kelly, poet, author and speaker

'This is great! I find that as I read this book I say "yes, that's who I am".'
Evan Riffee, Editor, Connections, the journal of the World Evangelical Alliance Missions Commission

'Very thought-provoking. Having pastored a church in which were found 150 GenXers, I could identify with many of the issues and mindsets this book exposes.'
David Lundy, International Director, Arab World Ministries

'This book gives GenXers who are passionate about world mission the opportunity to look at it from their viewpoint. Both heartening and disturbing, and essential reading for all involved in mission peronnnel issues.'
Review in *Share*, the magazine of the South American Mission Society

'This is an exceedingly valuable book and should be compulsory reading for all mission executives and personnel staff.'
Stanley Davies, Executive Director, Global Connections

'I purchased several copies. My wife and I read it and were greatly impressed. My organisation's president's wife said "Finally, I can understand my own son better!" '
Rick Cruse, European Director, OC International

'This book could do much to widen a crucial debate about world mission. It is about the authors' struggles, and those of their peers, to find a place within mission agencies.'
Review in *Yes*, the magazine of the Church Mission Society

'A refreshing and insightful contribution by ten mission thinkers in their 20s and 30s.'
Stan Nussbaum, GMI

PostMission

World Mission by a Postmodern Generation

Edited by Richard Tiplady

PATERNOSTER PRESS

Contents

Foreword

Many of them had come out of paganism. They were not drawn to hierarchy or to great structures. They lived close to a creation they loved. They were open to the empowering presence of the Spirit and lived in the reality of signs and wonders. In their veins flowed a strange wanderlust, which they called *peregrinatio*: a form of pilgrimage. They travelled over land and sea, sailing even beyond the boundaries of their imagined world.

These were the Celtic Christians who saved Western civilization. These passionate Christian Celts became purposeful wanderers who took the incarnated Gospel into every corner of their emerald island. They sent their young and old, women and men, out in small bands to take the name of their beloved Christ into the ferocious tribal territories of the Picts (northern Scotland), major regions of England, what today is France, Switzerland, Italy, even the Ukraine. Their structure was unstructured: they lived in community; equipped in community; sent out their evangelizing teams from the community; and later welcomed many of them back to tell their stories of the advance of the Gospel of Christ. Today, places like Iona and Lindisfarne (Holy Island) are pilgrimage sites, but there are many other locations we could speak of.

In March 2001 a small band of dedicated Christians, seventeen members of the younger generation radically committed to world mission, gathered on Holy Island. They came from England, Ireland, New Zealand, Sweden, the USA and Canada. Amongst them was a couple from an older generation, present as 'elders', to listen, to speak when invited, to contribute to the worship and prayer and to the rich flow of discussion. It was no coincidence that the Generation Xers in Mission Roundtable met at Holy Island, a tidal island saturated with sacred history: to this day devout Christians, indebted to their Celtic heritage, sustain many rich Celtic traditions, plumbing ancient wisdom to face the challenges of modern society and postmodern cultural changes.

We were that older couple, and we were honoured to be there. In the providence of God, Richard Tiplady had approached me (Bill) in November 1999 during the Iguassu Missiological Consultation (convened by the Missions Commission, World Evangelical Alliance) about the possibility of calling together a group of younger mission leaders. Creativity flowed during that conversation. Potential names of participants were suggested, Richard volunteered to provide the initial leadership, and his organization at that time, Global Connections (the UK world mission network), released him to the project. It was then that I suggested the group meet on Holy Island. Thus was born the 'Holy Island Roundtable'.

As we evaluate this creative younger generation of mission leader, it is evident that they share some similar characteristics to Celtic Christians. We pray they will make a mark on their own complex and textured multicultural world as the Celts did on theirs.

The modern mission movement is undergoing a massive leadership transition. Too easily we talk in North America about generational categories (Builders, Boomers, Xers, Millennials) as if they are world-wide realities set in stone. The fact is that the marketing industry is segmenting these groups for profit, and they are doing it well. But whether there are two, three or four generational groups, the fact is that the mission movement is witnessing the transition from older to younger leaders that is taking place. Not surprisingly, many of the older leaders are unwilling to relinquish their hold (stranglehold?) on the mission infrastructure, and they have no intention of turning over control and power. Thankfully, other older and wiser heads have read the times, discerned the burgeoning creativity and commitment of younger leaders, and are fully engaged in the changeover.

It must also be said that in none of our Western cultures is there but one stream of younger leaders ('Generation Xers', or whatever label you use). This is true in society as well as within the Christian church and its global mission movement.

A few years ago, after Bill spoke at a North American mission leaders' meeting on the topic of attrition of long-term missionaries, a thirty-two-year-old Canadian asked to speak with him. He was blunt: 'Do you really think these agencies are going to open space for Generation Xers?' It was a tough question, and this was the response at the time.

The younger generation interested in world mission is diverse, and this may be a good thing. There are those who will fit into the existing structures because that is what they have known and are comfortable with. They will serve the systems and patterns of the past. They come from the more conservative churches, schools and mission organizations, and they include many missionary kids who want to return to a mythical world of their childhood.

A second group will find space in church and mission societies that give them latitude to be, to do, to create, to fail. Some agencies are actively recruiting the more restless Xers as a qualitatively different kind of mission candidate. They are willing to risk human, financial and organizational resources to see what God might want to do.

Yet a third group simply won't find room in established organizations. Many of them will create their own new mission structures and/or networks. In a sense they will mirror what a number of Boomers did in the USA perhaps twenty years ago: they will start their own thing, and recruit from their own like-minded generation. Another subset of these leaders will have served for a short- to mid-length period with existing organizations, then leave to start something new, or serve as mission consultants, or find another creative way to impact their world. They will remain committed to multifaceted world mission.

Yet a fourth group will serve through their churches, and this is a significant phenomenon we observe across the world. Churches are rightfully taking hold of the helm of their mission vision, and they are working in at least two directions. First, the church is the seedbed for recruitment and equipping of their own; they are sending, supporting and attempting to provide field-based strategizing and shepherding for these servants. The jury is still out as to whether churches can become 'full-service' sending bodies, and some of the early signs cause concern. Other signs are very encouraging. Secondly, churches are building partnerships and strategic alliances with field-based churches and ministries, whether international or national in origin and leadership. And in both cases the younger generations find creative space to be and to do.

Finally, there will be those who will serve solo, on their own. They may be the most restless younger entrepreneurs; they may become global Internet web masters; they may invest their human and financial resources to break through into some of the greatest creativity. Some will go bust. Hopefully they will recover and start again, never losing their passion for Christ and his global community.

We were privileged to become part of the Holy Island Roundtable as an elder sister and brother, a woman and a man, a couple with thirty-four years of marriage and ministry, parents of three creative and restless Xers ourselves. Providentially, Yvonne's decade-long study of Celtic Christianity flowed during those days of the Roundtable. We were honoured. We are impressed with this younger generation of mission leader.

On that basis we invite you to engage with the thoughts and implications of this book. Some of you might want to fasten your seat belts, for the ride may challenge presuppositions, structures, long-honoured ideas and systems. But rest assured, and do believe us. These women and men who gathered on Holy Island passionately love the Triune God and are dedicated to the singularity of the Gospel of Jesus for all cultures – whether generational, world view (that is, shaped by postmodernity), ethnic or whatever.

Bill and Yvonne Taylor

Introduction: Losing my religion?

Richard Tiplady

It is widely recognized that the West is experiencing a significant culture change. Estimates of its nature and importance vary, but it is undeniable that new generations are growing up with a world view radically different to that of their parents and grandparents. The label 'Generation X' has been applied to those born since the early–mid-1960s, and, by their attitudes and outlook, this generation shows itself to be the first to have been significantly shaped by postmodernity rather than by modernity.

Anecdotal evidence of the personal experience of 'Xers' shows that we do not find it easy to fit into the culture and structures of much of the contemporary Western church, especially in its organizational forms, such as mission agencies. As postmodernity is a reaction against modernity, so much of the Xer outlook is a reaction against the 'Baby-Boomer' world view that preceded it, and which currently shapes much of the organizational form and culture of Western society, including the church.

This mismatch has been noted by many 'Boomers' and older members of the world mission community and has led to some discussion of the 'problem' of Generation X and attempts to 'help' Xers to fit into existing cultural norms and structures. But what if the problem is not with the Xers? What if the problem is with the culture of the existing structures? If mission agencies, in their structures, procedures and ethos, reflect the world view of the generations that formed them, then these are not sacrosanct. Like all cultural forms, they are contingent, relative and subject to evaluation by other cultural norms and by the Bible.

If Generations Xers do world mission their way, again subject to evaluation by the Bible and by others, but in a way that is true to their own world view none the less, what would it look like? Are new strategies, structures and methodologies needed? Can the existing structures be changed to allow the Xer world view to exist alongside others, or are new ones needed?

So began a proposal that circulated informally by word of mouth (or word of e-mail) among Generation Xers with leadership responsibilities in mission agencies. It resulted in a meeting, lasting five days, held at Holy Island (Lindisfarne), a tidal island off the north-east coast of England. At this gathering, seventeen Generation X mission leaders from the UK, USA, Canada, Sweden and New Zealand spent time sharing their stories, ideas, joys and frustrations. We discussed common issues, trends and models, and decided that we wanted to initiate a wider discussion about the above issues, among both our peers and our seniors.

This book, written entirely by some of those present at Holy Island, is one outcome of that meeting.

When Michael Stipe of REM sang the words to the song 'Losing my religion' he articulated a sense of disillusion with the church felt by many not just of his generation, but by Generation Xers too. (So powerful has this metaphor been that an entire book has been built around it.)[1] Awareness of this sense of disillusionment with the church and its various organizational structures, such as mission agencies, is nothing new. The seminal article on this issue from a mission agency perspective appeared as long ago as 1997,[2] and considerable hot air has been expended on the issue since.

---

[1] Tom Beaudoin, *Virtual Faith* (San Francisco: Jossey Bass Wiley, 1998).
[2] Kath Donovan and Ruth Myors, 'Reflections on Attrition in Career Missionaries: A Generational Perspective into the Future' in William D. Taylor (ed.), *Too Valuable To Lose* (Pasadena, California: William Carey Library, 1997).

And yet anecdotal evidence shows that many Xers in mission agencies feel alone, or at best isolated, in the struggles and disillusion they feel towards the very structures that are meant to be supporting them in their work. This disillusion does not extend to Jesus Christ, nor to their sense of calling to Christian mission. But an increasing number of Generation Xer missionaries are coming to the conclusion that the struggle with the organizational culture and structures within which they are expected to work is just not worth it, and they are 'opting out', returning home, and finding new ways of serving Jesus Christ in their local communities. From a mission agency perspective, however, these people disappear off the radar screen and are written off as 'quitters'. There seems to be a painful lack of self-awareness among many of the 'power holders' in the world mission movement, with few asking whether the problem might just be with them, not with the Xers.

We're not weird, and we don't have horns

One of the purposes of the small international get-together that we called the 'Holy Island Roundtable' was to bring together some of those Xers who had not yet reached the point of no return. Most were still trying to find a way of making it work within the established mission agency structures. The most exciting things I heard during our first morning together, as we began to get to know each other and listen to one another's stories, were comments like 'I didn't know other people felt like this' and 'I thought I was just weird, and that it was all my fault.' Aside from the therapy-group dynamics of these disclosures, they increased within us the awareness that these tensions are not just a temporary or isolated phenomenon, but are in fact manifestations of broader cultural changes in the West (and perhaps the world). And we are convinced that these changes are not just something external to the church, but are in fact something in which we all share and are deeply involved.

This is an important point to emphasize at the start. This is *not* something that is external to the church. It cannot be ignored, wished away, or written off as something to do with 'the world'. It is part of the air we all breathe. The language and culture of postmodernity provides us with a way to describe and analyse the cognitive dissonance felt by many, as well as perhaps being one of the causes of that dissonance. A simplistic reaction would tell us that it is therefore a simple matter of 'not conforming to the world',[3] and offering obedient submission to the leadership of one's mission organization. But we don't think that the culture of the mission agencies is more Christian than that of postmodernity. The middle section of this book – 'The end of the world as we know it' – asks whether the very opposite might, in some cases, be true? Is God, through postmodernity, offering us new ways of thinking and behaving that will help us to shake off the cultural captivity of modernity, to which evangelicalism is perhaps particularly prone?

We want to ask whether the supposedly 'classic' missionary attitudes of flexibility, longevity of service and subordination and obedience to one's leaders are in fact more a reflection of the culture of those who shaped the modern Christian missionary movement after World War II rather than being especially Christian as such.[4] Like all other cultures, therefore, they are relative and bound to certain times and places. They too shall pass.

There is a tension between who we as Generation Xers understand ourselves to be and the places we have tried to 'fit into' (the mission agencies). Neither culture can be said to be specifically Christian, and so we are trying to find a 'third place' – 'Christians in a postmodern culture'. We do not want to baptize postmodernity and call it Christian, but neither do we consider it something to be merely repented of. We want to be countercultural, and to critique our own culture from a Christian perspective, but this is not the same thing as just conforming to the 'missionary' culture (or any other culture). The bottom line is

---

[3] Based on a sound bite misquote of Romans 12:2.
[4] For a practical analysis of the generational cultural differences that support this assertion see R. Zemke, C. Raines and B. Filipczak, *Generations At Work* (New York: Amacom, 2000).

that we believe postmodernity, like all other cultures, is to be redeemed by the Gospel of Jesus Christ. In short, using missionary jargon, a work of contextualization has to be done. And contextualization is never done best when the missionaries do it – it is the locals who have to do it. And so, while we welcome outside input (as we did at Holy Island, where we welcomed Bill Taylor, Director of WEA [World Evangelical Alliance] Missions Commission, and his wife, Yvonne, to be with us as 'older brother and sister'), we have to do this task for ourselves.

So, in this book we begin to ask what contextually appropriate ways of doing mission need to exist for a postmodern generation and for those that follow us.

One of the answers we came up with at Holy Island was that there will not be only one single way of doing mission, nor perhaps even a dominant one. Within us as a group there were those who wanted to work within their existing mission organization to help bring about change. Others wanted to explore whether there could be new organizational forms for mission involvement. Some wanted to involve local churches more closely. Others didn't. Diversity is the word we chose to describe this. Rather than a 'missionary sausage machine', where all the 'bits' (dregs?) are mixed up together, forced to fit a standard size and all look the same, we want to see a situation where variety and diversity are not just accepted, but welcomed as something positive.

We also want to break the cycle of the past, where one generation seized power from another. During our time together, at first tentatively, then with increasing confidence, people shared their belief that they, as Generation Xers, were part of a transitional generation. We don't want to perpetuate the cycle of irrelevance that stems from holding on to power when the world has moved on. This may come as a surprise to older generations, especially the Baby-Boomers. Personally, I feel a degree of sympathy for the Baby-Boomers, who since the sixties have viewed themselves as cultural innovators. Sorry, guys. The world has moved on. The tide has gone out, and you're looking a bit high and dry.

I had a revealing conversation about this cycle of power grab-
bing with Pete Broadbent, now Anglican Bishop of Willesden in
England, a few years ago. He confided in me that his generation,
the Baby-Boomers, had taken power from their seniors in the
sixties and seventies, and that they were now waiting for the
Generation Xers to do the same to them. As we showed no strong
inclination to do so, they were carrying on enjoying themselves
running things. When I told Pete that most Generation Xers don't
really care about seizing power, and so will just let the Baby-
Boomers carry on running things while the world goes in a
different direction, he showed considerable surprise! So let's be
clear about this. It's not power that we want. Postmodern ideas
have given us the tools to see power for what it is, and frankly, it's
not attractive. We don't want it. What we're concerned about is
justice and the equality that we believe will come through an
honest commitment to diversity. And in this the role of Generation Xers might be simply to 'break up the ground', to prepare the
way for succeeding generations.

E *pluribus unum*? Or is the sausage machine the only way?

The above Latin phrase ('from many, one') is used to describe the
'melting pot' philosophy of the United States, which has united its
many and diverse immigrant groups in the common identity of
being 'American'. Many believe that a single uniting cultural
metaphor is vital if people are going to work together effectively:

> Although some companies have tried it, one thing that can't be
> internationalised is organisational culture. For individuals, national
> culture is a strong element of identity, providing a framework of
> assumptions within which others' reactions can be anticipated and
> judged.[5]

---

[5] Simon Caulkin in *The Observer*, 25 July 1999.

The first essential of organisational efficiency is cultural purity. To each his own god. Harmony is health. It is when the gods compete within one activity that confusion results.[6]

If these statements are true, they might equally be taken to apply to other forms of cultural diversity, such as the different generations, which is the interest of this book. But are they actually right?

Most organizations (like most churches) tend to be fairly homogeneous. Like attracts like. People are attracted to, and recruited by, organizations that appear to have values and an outlook fairly similar to their own. Those who do not fit in usually leave. There are several good reasons why this happens:

- Recruitment practices emphasize finding people through sources that have been historically reliable (in other words, we only look in the same places).
- Selection practices stress choosing candidates similar to those who have been successful (of course, the missionary priorities and context of the early twenty-first century are very different to those of the mid-1960s).[7]
- Training programmes tend to promote uniform ways of thinking (although a healthy dose of adult-learning principles can correct this).
- Supervisors are often limited in the extent to which they can address an individual's unique needs.[8]

In a sector that has numerous niche operators, each different to the other, this doesn't matter too much, because people eventually gravitate towards a place they feel at home. But the Western missionary movement, for all its long history, doesn't have that

---

[6] Charles Handy, *The Gods Of Management* (London: Arrow, 1995).
[7] Donovan and Myors, 'Reflections on Attrition in Career Missionaries', p. 52.
[8] Zemke, Raines and Filipczak have an excellent section on changing this practice in *Generations At Work*, pp. 153–9.

many different niches. Some newer organizations (those formed since the end of World War II) might be slightly different in some ways from the older mission agencies that began existence in the late (or early) nineteenth century. But the niche organizations for Xers are not that thick on the ground. Xers haven't really started that many mission agencies yet. It would be good if the existing organizations could change before it becomes necessary for Xers to repeat the pattern of history and start up too many new organizations just because they rejected, and were rejected by, the existing structures.

I believe that diversity is a God-intended reality for his people. Archbishop Desmond Tutu came up with the remarkable phrase 'the rainbow people of God' that was a vision for racial reconciliation in South Africa. The 'homogeneous unit principle' has been a bone of contention within the missionary movement since the phrase was first coined. Many oppose it as a method of church growth, despite its pragmatic advantages, because it just doesn't fit with the belief that in Christ God has destroyed the 'dividing wall of hostility' (Ephesians 2:14) and has reconciled humanity not just to himself, but to one another. But if it's not OK for churches to be like that, why should it be any different for organizations that claim to be Christian?

I also believe, however, that diversity is not just an end in itself (however important that may be). It is also a means to an end. Among the reasons why organizations that are diverse in generational mix (as well as ethnicity and gender) will be more effective in world mission are:

- Xers themselves are a diverse group. We resist categorization. I am not, and do not wish to be, a target market. None the less, organizations that genuinely exhibit diversity will have a much bigger pool of recruits within which to fish, whose varied contributions will then enhance the effectiveness and impact of that organization in its work and life.
- Globalization is making the world a more complex place. There are still a few remote homogeneous tribal groups in the world (and thank God for those mission organizations

committed to working among them). But most of the world is urbanizing rapidly, and these urban inhabitants have an increasing number of choices available about their identity and world view. We live in a consumer-oriented world that has moved from *mass-production* to *mass-customization*. A diverse missionary workforce will have much greater impact on these diverse urban populations than the product of a 'sausage machine' ever could.

This book does exactly what it says on the cover

This book sets out to assist this process of diversification. It is written for both the existing leadership of the Western missionary movement, and for those emerging Xer leaders who experience some of the tensions described above. It aims to do three things:

1. To build understanding of the outlook of Generation Xers across the world mission sector. This book is not the first to do this, nor will it be the last. But most of these books are not written by Xers. They are written *about* us. This book is written *by* us. We want to give expression to our own understanding of our self-identity, not have someone else do it for us.
2. To suggest that postmodernity, as the cultural environment by which Western Generation Xers have been considerably shaped, in not *necessarily* the end of all things good, holy and true, and *might actually* be an opportunity for the church to recover some of the things it lost in its struggle with modernity.
3. To provide ideas and models for systemic organizational culture change, for without this, goodwill and mutual understanding will only do half the job required.

Thus the book is split into three sections, each relating to one of the above aims. Following the title of this chapter (and with apologies to Michael Stipe), each section has the title of an REM song. Actually, I tried to think of a way to use other REM songs such as 'What's the frequency, Kenneth?' and 'The sidewinder sleeps tonight' as section titles, but I couldn't.

Any astute reader will notice quite a diversity of style within this book. There is passion and anger, born out of frustration and hurt, and there is also some more dispassionate analysis. Initially I was concerned about this, until someone pointed out to me that it reflects one of the main points we're trying to make – Generation X is diverse, and you just have to deal with it. Whatever.

About the contributors

Carolyn Cole – Carolyn was first inspired into mission at the age of sixteen, in Peru. After university she taught geography in a secondary school and then did a gap year with Oasis Trust in London. She went to Bible College at All Nations Christian College and spent three years on the mission field in Brazil with Latin Link and Youth With A Mission. She then trained mission volunteers with the Baptist Missionary Society and now train overseas missionaries in YWAM.

Joanne Goode – Having spent six years speeding around the UK and sending off numerous teams to Africa as Africa Inland Mission UK's Youth Worker, Joanne now works as Associate Director for Christian Vocations, a UK agency that helps channel people into various forms of Christian work. She is known by most people as 'the wee curly-haired Irish one'.

Paula Harris – Paula's day job is developing content and herding speakers, musicians and actors for the Urbana Student Missions Convention. She is growing as a missiologist and enjoys writing and teaching about reconciliation, cultural identity and post-modern culture. She has two kids – her dream is that they grow up loving Jesus, people of other cultures, and themselves.

Rob Hay – Rob is a management consultant and member of the Institute of Directors. Until recently he was Health Services

Director for International Nepal Fellowship, where he managed a team of forty-five people from fifteen nations, covering thirteen professional areas, spread across seven geographical locations. He survived by having a great (and gracious) team and drinking copious amounts of sweet Nepalese tea. Now he and Sarah have returned from Nepal to undertake a three-year research project on missionary attrition. He is also the very proud dad of one-year-old Thomas.

Sarah Hay – Sarah is a professional personnel manager by training and an amateur mum in training. A member of the Institute for Personnel and Development, Sarah worked in roles in the public and commercial sectors before doing the Professionals in Mission course at Redcliffe College. Recently she and husband Rob returned from Nepal, where she was the Personnel Manager for International Nepal Fellowship, responsible for personnel and member care of 200 expatriate staff. Now, in between looking after Thomas, she is working on a research project on missionary attrition.

Bevan Herangi – Until 1999, Bevan was involved in local church and community youth work, running groups and events. Since then he has worked for Open Doors in New Zealand, mainly raising awareness for the persecuted church around the Christian youth/young adult population. Bevan loves seeing people experience personal breakthroughs while participating in outdoors adventures and global mission trips.

Peter Stephenson – Peter designed bridges for a few years, then got tired of concrete and became a missionary in Spain instead (there was a bit more to it than that – a call, and so on), working in drug rehabilitation and church planting. His interests include mountain walking, photography, enjoying his family, a decent pint, and the need to change the way we think about and do mission.

Bill Taylor – Bill and Yvonne Taylor have been married for thirty-five years, and have three Generation X children, all born in

Guatemala. Bill was born in Costa Rica, the son of missionaries, and lived in Latin America for thirty years, seventeen of them with Yvonne in Guatemala. He has a ThM in theology from Dallas Seminary and a PhD in Latin American studies from the University of Texas, Austin. Since 1986 Bill has been the Executive Director of the World Evangelical Alliance Missions Commission and has edited numerous books on world mission, including *Global Missiology for the 21st Century: The Iguassu Dialogue* (Grand Rapids, Michigan: Baker, 2000).

Yvonne Taylor – Yvonne is a native Texan with a university degree in liberal arts/music. Living and working for thirty-five years in Latin America and other international cross-cultural settings, she is Bill's full partner in ministry as a critical thinker, sounding board and editor. A long-time student of Christian spirituality in the historic streams of Christianity, God's calling on Yvonne is to minister in spiritual formation and spiritual direction. Bill and Yvonne attend Hope Chapel in their city of Austin, Texas.

Richard Tiplady – Richard works as an organizational development consultant, specializing in innovation, new projects and organizational change. Clients include Oasis Trust, Global Connections, WEA Missions Commission, and others. Prior to this, from 1996 to 2002 Richard was Associate Director of Global Connections, the UK evangelical network for world mission, with a particular interest in organizational development, new initiatives, and the changing face of mission during a postmodern transition. A qualified Football Association junior football coach, Richard is married to Irene, who works with people with long-term mental health problems, and they have one son, Jamie, age ten.

Part 1

Shiny happy people
(Who do Generation Xers think they are?)

1

So, like, what's with these Xers, man?

How do Generation Xers understand themselves?
What are our core values?

Bevan Herangi

Each generation has its own set of values that influence their world view. Clashes of world view happen when one generation can't see where the other is coming from.

Dale Carnegie, who is known as the pioneer of personal skills development in the West, taught millions of people through training sessions and books how to be successful in all areas of life. One of the keys he used to teach people was to try and look at an issue from another person's point of view. On this subject he wrote:

> Remember that other people may be totally wrong. But they don't think so. Don't condemn them. Any fool can do that. Try to understand them. Only wise, tolerant, exceptional people even try to do that. There is a reason why the other man thinks and acts as he does. Ferret out that reason – and you have the key to his actions, perhaps to his personality.[1]

---

[1] Dale Carnegie, *How To Win Friends And Influence People* (London: Vermillion, 1998), p. 171.

The purpose of this chapter is to give you a glimpse into why we Xers are the way we are. There are actually reasons for our outlook on life and the way we think, act and react. We have a set of core values that influence our every direction, whether good or bad. It is important to note that several of the values seem to contradict one another. Don't be too worried about that: it's just the diverse nature of the Xer generation showing through.

We want to be ourselves, and develop our own identity

Of the many things discussed at the Holy Island Roundtable, I distinctly remember the analogy of the 'sausage machine', where all kinds of mixtures and ingredients were put in one end, and, after a big mix up, a whole batch of identical sausages would pop out the other end. Though it was used in a humorous way to describe the type of production system that many mission agencies use to produce new missionaries in its particular 'shape and flavour', it really struck a nerve with most of us. Behind the laughing, each of us loathed the thought of being squashed into being something we were not. Many felt the sausage machine was not only used by mission organizations but by society in general. Parents with good intentions pushed us to excel in areas that they understood to be successful for life. Friends and schoolmates put pressure on us to conform to their ideals, which were basically identical to whatever fad was being pumped out by the secular media culture at the time. Even in a church setting we were pressured into being the 'model Christian', in many cases a geeky, irrelevant model that represented anything but Christlikeness. Many Xers have felt pressured to conform to be something they are not, whether by family, friends, media, culture or church/ mission agency.

When I left school at the early age of fifteen, I was encouraged to work in a trade, painting and decorating being the one I took up. I was encouraged to get through my apprenticeship, work really hard, get married, save up a deposit for a house, get a loan, and then work to pay the bank off. This was what everybody did.

Somehow you reached success when you owned your own home. The media pushed it; friends and family encouraged you towards it. So the mere thought of working in another country for a Christian mission or even a local voluntary movement, where wages were low or other people supported you, was and is somewhat against the grain. 'Get a real job!' 'How will you live?' 'Are you saving for a house?' Though these ideals aren't evil themselves, they represent a mindset that is biased against those that feel called to something else.

Several descriptions have been used to try and identify the 'X' of Generation X, but we are such a diverse bunch that nothing really sticks. It could be said that we desire to be all things to all people. In a mission context, we see this value as being key for reaching a diverse, postmodern world.

We're flexible and like our freedom

There is no doubt that we love to be flexible. To many Xers, work is only a means to an end; that is, we work to live, not the other way around. We don't see the problem with working from 10 a.m. to 3 p.m. so that we can spend more time doing some other activity that we like. We will even pay others to do certain jobs (for example the gardening and the housework) so we can spend more time with friends, family or a sports team. We also involve our play with our work (doing what we love to do and getting paid for it). Professional sport has really taken off in the last ten to fifteen years. What was just a sport can now be a career. A lot of Xers are getting a lot of money for running with a ball.

Xers don't hold on to family or cultural laws as tightly as Boomers did. It is not uncommon in families for the woman to work and for the man to stay at home looking after the kids. Ten to fifteen years ago it would have been shameful if the man, the 'provider', earned less money than his wife, the 'homemaker'.

For us, if it works, then let's do it. We witnessed the 'wealth pursuit' of the eighties and saw Boomers sacrifice families, friends, personal health and even faith for the enticement of money. We saw the effects of burnout hit many who were striving to make it big, and asked, 'Is it all worth it?' We value our freedom more than the trappings of money. Boomers believed they were free because they had 'freedom to choose': 'I can choose to pursue money at the expense of family and health.' We believe we are free when we make choices that bring us into a state of freedom: 'I choose to preserve the things I love in life at the expense of not becoming rich.'

We seek out new experiences and positive change

Xers have been at the forefront of extreme sports and recreation development in the West. We are seekers of the 'New Experience'. Bungee jumping started in New Zealand in the late eighties and became the new adrenaline for Xers. Since then dozens more extreme sports have emerged, and we now have the 'X Games' in the States, which draw people from all over the world to be part of 'the experience'. We don't just want to see professionals doing their stuff – we want to have a go at it. 'If they can do it then I must be able to as well!'

Reality TV is huge in the West, showing real footage of Xers' reactions to challenges and relational issues. Xers are big on travelling and love experiencing the diverse cultures that the world has to offer. We desire to have a positive effect on those who are in need, and many desire to serve in missions or volunteer services.

If one of my friends bought a new motorbike, I never thought about how nice it looked or sounded, but what it would be like for me to ride on. When I hear of associates taking bibles and aid into dangerous countries, where you have to walk for days through dense jungles, dodging armed terrorists groups and meeting with secret believers, I don't think about how hard it must have been for them: I visualize myself doing it too.

Us Xers don't want to sit back in the realm of couch potatoes, switching channels: we want to be out in the field having a go. We love to see positive change, especially when it involves people that we have had contact with. I remember sponsoring a child through World Vision a few years back. I had the child's picture on my wall and would write letters to her. One day I was told that my support had achieved a good standard of living for her and her project was finished. That type of thing really gets us going!

We are adaptable

In a world of constant change, we are not so concerned or fearful that tomorrow the world may change again. We find it easy to adapt to situations and forget what it was like before. Where Boomers in the West were raised in a predominantly Christian era and are shocked at every secular advancement in the world, we were brought up by the 'post-Christian', secular media, which has taught us to put up with anything. Therefore we get on with life in almost any situation and just adapt. When things change, we just change too. Living in a computer age, we don't fear what the future technology will be, because each new technology teaches us how to use it. We just adapt.

We are plagued by self-doubt, and are questioning of our and others' abilities

Though excited about new possibilities or promotions we tend to be a bit self-doubting of our abilities to step up to the mark: 'The task is achievable but I'm not sure if I can do it – what if I stuff it up?' We need encouragement and affirmation that we *can* do it. Many Xers have a fear of failure and accredit this to their own lack of development. We also shy away from taking top honours, preferring others to take the glory, or to receive it only in a team setting. Maybe we feel we never measured up, or something?

This is in real contrast to our enthusiasm for entrepreneurial, risk-taking activities. We see our self-doubt as a kind of safety net that stops us getting too successful and then falling from a height. Having seen the rise and fall of so many great people, we tend to want to take the low road, or at least go as a group, so fame doesn't rest on one person alone.

When involved in cross-cultural evangelism, we tend to shy away from promoting our own lifestyle as being superior to others, as we are not confident that we actually have the right answers for them. We want to preach Jesus, not our Western philosophy or ideals.

We desire truth, reality and authenticity

Even if it means a painful experience, we must know the truth. Unlike other generations that swept a lot of misdemeanours under the rug, we want to face the facts. We don't just believe what people say, we wait and see what they live. Never have leaders of churches or countries come under so much scrutiny as they have from Generation Xers. We don't want to hear the positive propaganda of the rich and famous: we want the real-life stories of normal people who come from normal families. My wife works for one of the biggest 'women's magazines' in New Zealand. It has kept a very high readership through the years because it contains a large amount of real-life stories. Prime-time television now features a whole bunch of reality TV programmes that show real people and real-life reactions to the challenges they face.

During the eighties and nineties a number of Christian leaders were caught committing adultery and were fired. It was discovered that some of these people had been 'doing it' for years. So, on the one hand, they taught Christian values and inspired people to live for God, and, on the other, they lived immoral lifestyles. Many people were fully disillusioned and left the churches because they were not real or authentic. Xers have left the church in droves because it lost its edge in presenting the real Gospel of Jesus. The cause of the Gospel, seeing people saved, was replaced by much teaching of the theory of Christianity. This bores us, as we value an experiential faith.

In the closing scenes of the movie *Braveheart*, William Wallace (Mel Gibson), stretched out on the torture rack with all his joints dislocated, is given the option of pleading for mercy from the king. To do so would mean giving up the cause he had lived for: the freedom of Scotland from English rule. With the whole crowd yelling 'Mercy! Mercy!' and individuals praying he would ask for mercy, William Wallace, now disemboweled, motions his mouth to speak. The executioner signals to the crowd to be silent, shouting that the traitor has something to say. Silence falls as Wallace, with his last breath, shouts 'Freeeedom!!' He was real and practised what he preached, even to the point of death. This is what Jesus is to Xers too, but the Western church doesn't see it. Christian Xers desire to live like Jesus; fully committed to his cause.

We desire 'input' in our lives

Xers are fully open to caring, one-on-one, personal mentoring by stable, secure people. In fact, even though it may seem that 'we don't need anybody', we literally hang out for coaching, and, even more than that, fathering. We want someone to come along-side us and have input, give directions and keep us accountable. Many Xers have an inner search for the father or boundary-setter that was never there – someone to nudge us beyond our own experiences and walk with us through places they have been.

Recently I spent three weeks travelling with an Open Doors guest speaker. This man had spent forty years in Christian minis-try, compared to my three years. Every day, as we drove from town to town, he would share his experiences, the amazing achievements, terrible failures, and the lessons he learnt from God. He answered my many, many questions, shared personal hopes and dreams, and challenged my motives and attitudes. As you can imagine, by the time we parted company, I was a different man. He had been mentoring me, and it changed my life … just ask my wife. I wished he could stay longer and have more input.

We desire to have input from confident role models who are not afraid to be transparent or give us a dose of truth when we need it. We don't want people telling us what to do, but advising us on choices and consequences. But we don't want too many choices or options (just to confuse things). What we desire is understanding and input from people committed to sharing their experiences, both successes and failures, and lessons learnt.

We're sceptical and cynical, and find it hard to trust others

Through life experiences we have learnt to question everything, including the principles, laws and ideals of the previous generations. Moreover, we are very sceptical when future prospects are proclaimed or promises made. In the past people just believed what was promised, and said nothing if it didn't come into being. False prophets were able to carry on their merry way. In contrast, Xers tend to throw the baby out with the bath water: 'Stone the prophets!' (even if what they said came true).

We like to set aside an escape route if things don't turn out the way that was promised: we don't commit fully to schemes or visions of other people. We tend to look out for number one, because everybody else has got an agenda. 'What do they really want from me?', we question.

Growing up through the cold war period of the seventies and eighties, espionage, scandals, CIA dealings and secret agents like 007 all contributed to the general feeling that you could trust no one. Not even World War II allies. The Americans seemed to have their own agenda. Were the Russians really as bad as the papers made them out to be? What about all this Contra Deal stuff? And did they really land on the moon? Xers have been landed with too many unanswered questions, and as a result we have developed antitrust radars that sound an alarm whenever there is information, news, promises or prophecy directed our way. Xers take all great claims with a grain of salt, and, after seeing many future claims come to nothing, don't like to overproject for fear of underproducing.

We are tolerant and like diversity

We are very accepting of the views of others and open for sugges-
tion on our own. This doesn't mean we have a grey outlook on
life, but that we see the need for many colours, not just black and
white. If another person doesn't believe what we believe, then
that's their choice. We see others' right to freedom of belief; we
see our right to the same. We value the cultural input that many
other nationalities offer and are far more accepting of other races
living in our society than were previous generations. Xers are not
afraid to mix it as equals with people of different cultures.

Even in the context of evangelism, Xers tend to share their
faith more effectively when engaged in conversations that are
'two way', especially where personal beliefs, cultural philosophy
and ideals are concerned: we value the other person's thoughts on
faith issues as much as we want them to value ours. In New
Zealand the term 'Bible-basher' is used to describe a Christian
person who never gives the recipient of his or her revelation the
opportunity to defend their views. They talk over them, quote
Scripture and then condemn/write off the unsaved person if they
don't agree and convert. Even the mention of the word 'Bible-
basher' creates negative vibes in a secular group. Bigoted, unyielding, harsh, intolerant and extremist are some of the terms
used to describe them. As Dale Carnegie writes in his book *How
to Win Friends and Influence People*, 'If there is any one secret of
success, it lies in the ability to get the other person's point of view
and see things from that person's angle as well as from your
own.'[2]

On a negative note, we can be so tolerant of others' views and
behaviour that we fail to stand against and sometimes even
condone the propagation of un-Christian practices in our society.
Abortion, legalization of addictive drugs, introduction of same-
sex marriages, euthanasia, legal prostitution and pornography, to
name but a few, have increased rapidly in our generation. As

---

[2] Ibid. p. 58.

Polish philosopher Leszek Kolakowski noted, 'It is important to notice, however that when tolerance is enjoined upon us nowadays, it is often in a sense of indifference: We are asked in effect, to refrain from expressing – or indeed holding – any opinion, and sometimes even to condone every conceivable type of behaviour or opinion in others.'[3]

We value real leadership, not controlling authority

In their farewell tributes to Kiwi sailing hero and explorer the late Sir Peter Blake, those who had sailed with him on the round-the-world yacht races or UN environment expeditions said they would follow him anywhere, they trusted him and that he was a true leader. For many years, teams of young people would follow Brother Andrew, and smuggle bibles into the Soviet Union and other restrictive nations. Risking their lives with him, they sought out the persecuted church and encouraged them. Why would people commit to these men? Because they were true leaders who led with courage, and many people followed their lead.

Through abusive experiences or independent upbringing, Xers tend to see leadership in a different light. We've seen people sacrifice their families and friends in their quest for power or title in business or ministry. We have also served under leaders who think and act as though their authority means ultimate lordship. We value leadership, but not from people that lord it over us because of title or position. If they feel that they have to try and force us to follow them, they are not leaders. In the film *Braveheart* William Wallace stirs an unconfident Robert the Bruce by saying 'Men don't follow titles, they follow courage.' At the end of the film, many Scots follow Robert the Bruce into battle against the English. He leads them in the charge.[4]

---

[3] Alex Buchan, *Quotes To Live By* (Streetsville, Ontario: Open Doors International, 2001), p. 13.
[4] J. Martin Wood, The X-Cultural Mission Challenge seminar papers (unpublished).

I recently talked with a sheep farmer in the south of New Zealand and asked how he rounded up so many sheep when shearing time came. He said it was simple – all he would do was open the gate, call out to them, and they would all come running to him and follow him to the wool shed. There was no rushing around or stressing out – he would search for any stragglers or sick sheep, but the rest just followed him. Like those sheep, we are very open to following a leader who leads, but react when herded or forced to do something. We respond well when called, and follow good leadership well, especially when we are allowed to play our part and do what we do best. But we really react against enticement or force by leaders intent on shoving us through the sausage machine.

We love community, and thrive on that good old 'sense of belonging'

Predominantly in the West, the feeling of community has been lost over the last ten to twenty years, as people have sought to be in 'consumer competition' with their neighbours instead of caring for and supporting them. In New Zealand fencing contractors have been very busy indeed as homeowners have sought to keep their affairs private and their neighbours out! It would be very rare for people to *know* more than two of their neighbours, even after four to five years of living side by side. The same could be said for some church situations, where in large, 'happening' churches, fences are erected after the Sunday service and pulled down again before the next one. Though we live/worship in the midst of a multitude of people, we don't know them. This has caused us Xers to want something deeper than the general network of peers and associates. We will join sports clubs, hobby groups, prayer groups, gangs and so on just to get that community feel.

We feel free to be ourselves in a small community and let others be themselves without fuss. When in a group of close friends we let down our guard and relax. Even when there is some disagreement within a group, we will still tend to stay in it as it's an anchor for us.

It has been said that Boomers networked with a lot of people, whereas we spend a lot of time with a few people. My wife and I have a close-knit group of friends numbering around ten families. Though we are all busy in life with businesses, Christian ministry, families and so on, we see the need for gatherings – they are important in our relationships. We are always having parties, holidays, camps, dinners and adventures together. This seems to feed our need for belonging and being there for others.

We are an interesting generation with many positives and negatives to offer. It would be easier for everyone if we just conformed to the pattern of earlier generations: there wouldn't be the grating or struggles with modernity. But then I guess we wouldn't be the people God has lined up to reach our generation.

2

I still haven't found what I'm looking for

Why do Generation X struggle to find a place in mission agencies?

Peter Stephenson, Joanne Goode and Carolyn Cole

In the U2 song 'I still haven't found what I'm looking for' Bono sings of his struggle to find Christ in a church that was alien to him back in the late 1980s. It is a cry perhaps echoed by many mission workers in their twenties and thirties who are now trying to find their place in the strange world of Western mission agencies. In this chapter we seek to assess the causes behind the new generation's sense of disconnection with existing mission agencies. We also hope to identify the reasons why there are often huge tensions when young people do become mission workers – tensions that often result in premature departure from the mission field.

At the heart of these struggles is the profound sense of mismatch felt by many younger missionaries in established Western mission agencies, and indeed the reluctance of many would-be missionaries to commit themselves to an agency. As a potential missionary recruit in his early twenties wrote, 'the main problems I had with missions was that I felt like I was joining the army, everything was so 19th century. [Also] I felt like I could not sign up to such an organisation that I felt might suck me dry and leave me for dead. It's difficult but I find it hard to commit to people who I don't feel are committed to me.'[1]

---

[1] Personal correspondence, December 2001.

Many younger workers who do join established organizations find that they just do not fit in, and feel a constant pressure to conform in a way that creates many internal tensions. Some either can not or will not conform and so leave; others live under the constant strain of pretending to be who they are not in order to 'fit'; whilst others submit to the demands of the agency and become clones of their leaders, devoid of freshness and innovative potential.

This tension between mission leaders and younger people is not a uniquely Western problem, either. Despite the apparent (and often real) successes of the church and mission agencies in the two-thirds world, there is growing evidence that these same tensions are emerging in the non-Western church as the effects of globalized postmodernity has its effect on the younger genera-tions of those churches. As one of us recently heard a prominent and widely travelled African church leader say, 'Young people in the West and young people in Africa are now beginning to look the same.'[2] The issues that are raised in this paper, whilst focused on tensions between younger missionaries and Western missions agencies, may well be equally relevant in non-Western churches and mission agencies, either now or in the near future. Nor will these issues pass away in a few years. Says one recruitment director of a major missions agency:

> I'm concerned by the fact that Gen-Xers are beginning to get relatively old and we have another generation on its way in. I feel that I have a degree of understanding of Gen-Xers and that there are a good number of points where I identify with them, but I think there's a huge gap between me and the new generation. What I'm trying to say is, let's not think it's finished when [our agency] has become GenX-friendly because there's an even bigger challenge ahead of us.[3]

---

[2] Comment given at a recent conference discussion on Western culture change.
[3] Personal correspondence, April 2001.

The reality of the struggle: contours of conflict

Because of the shift from modernity to postmodernity, we would suggest that the very real tensions between mission agencies and Generation X missionaries are of a fundamentally different nature to previous generational tensions. What then are the main contours of these tensions? What are the world view conflicts that lead to tension? And is there any way to resolve the tensions? Missionary attrition rates, and the very inability of some traditional mission agencies to recruit and retain younger workers, suggest that the problems are grave, putting in doubt the future of many agencies. Young people, including Christians, are hungry for risk and adventure, are comfortable in the global village, and have a global vision and awareness unrivalled by previous generations. Missions should be an attractive proposition to postmodern Christians, and indeed the rapid growth of short-term programmes would bear this out. But the fact that, after a taste of short-term work, few Xers want to consider a missionary career should raise big questions for agencies. That so many of those who do opt for career missionary work return home prematurely should raise bigger questions still. What is going wrong?

The authors of this chapter currently work for three different agencies. Our mission experience is on three different continents. We have networked with many other Xers in different agencies and mission fields. Yet the tensions and conflicts that we and our peers have experienced are frighteningly similar, and all of them have roots in the cultural shift of which we are a part. We will now try to identify the main areas of tension, and suggest ways ahead. Lack of space prohibits us from being able to trace the roots of many of the areas of conflict between postmodern (predominantly younger) missionaries and their modernist (predominantly older) colleagues to the cultural transformation now taking place. We will limit ourselves to painting a broader picture of the realities we have experienced, seen and heard of from others. Those readers who have read more widely on post-modernity as a cultural rejection of all that modernity stood for will note how all these areas of conflict mirror the clash of cultures in the Western world in general. The stories we tell in this section are fictional, but are all based on real situations.

Attitudes to authority

Chris was still reeling from the fallout from a simple question he had asked his line manager in the mission's personnel department. In his usual open and frank manner, he had asked John (his superior) about his decision to assign of one of their new missionaries to a posting where he knew there were important unresolved problems that could subject missionaries to unnecessary risk and frustration. Chris felt he couldn't just sit back and watch his friend being taken advantage of. However, as soon as he raised the matter, it was clear that there was no opportunity for dialogue with John, who believed that Chris had overstepped the mark. In asking questions about assignments, Chris had strayed into territory that was 'none of his business'.

Hoping to clear the air, Chris decided to try to build bridges with his colleague, desiring to be transparent and accountable but without minimizing the problem. For him, restoring the relationship was of supreme importance. But Chris's attempts at reconciliation were met with a mixed response. On the one hand, it was agreed that they had to restore a good working relationship; but on the other hand, John made it clear that this restoration was conditional on Chris accepting John's terms and not questioning his decisions in any way.

This outcome hurt Chris perhaps more than a completely honest rejection would have. Whereas Chris had expected a warm response to his attempt to restore fellowship, he was met with a lukewarm pseudo-reconciliation on John's terms. Moreover, the whole issue was ignored by the head of personnel, who didn't want to appear to be taking sides, and so left John and Chris to sort it out between themselves. When this proved impossible, Chris was taken aside and warned not to disrespect those 'above him in the Lord'. Faced with conflict between his conscience and the mission's leadership ethos, Chris started to mentally compose his letter of resignation ...

- *Who was right?*
- *Could this difference have been resolved?*
- *Why did it occur in the first place?*

Modernist Christians have a generally positive attitude to authority figures, and missionaries are no exception. Christian leaders of dubious quality are usually given the benefit of the doubt, provided they do not transgress certain taboos such as sexual misconduct or financial embezzlement. It would be almost unthinkable to oppose a leader openly if they had not committed one or other of these taboos. Veteran and Boomer missionaries respect leaders who stand out from the crowd, who give the impression of being slightly aloof, above the level of ordinary Christians. One of us, on taking on a position of leadership in a missions agency, was advised by older colleagues to 'put a bit of distance between you and the others in the team – they will respect you more that way'.

Postmodern Christians do not share either this natural respect for leaders or a willingness to turn a blind eye to faults. To a certain degree, they will suffer poor leaders for a time, provided they do not cause too many difficulties, but they will not rally round a troubled leader in the same way as their predecessors would. Xer missionaries are often very aware of their own failings and have seen enough of the world to know that neither Christian nor secular leaders are much different to themselves, and so their attitude to leaders and authority in general is the opposite to that of their colleagues who are a decade or so older.

Whilst modernist Veteran/Boomer missionaries want and expect their leaders to be strong and confident, postmodern Xer missionaries want to see their leaders express an awareness of their own weaknesses and failings. They do not look so much for a hero or father/mother figure to act as a role model, but for someone who will stand with them and walk with them as a friend on their mutual journey to personal and spiritual maturity. They look for leaders humble enough to acknowledge that, far from having all the answers, they need the combined wisdom of all those who serve with them, regardless of age. Confident leaders who are seen by older workers as 'strong and assured in the Lord' are likely to be deemed by younger workers as arrogant and full of themselves. That does not mean that leaders have to be weak and without opinions, but rather that they must be genuinely humble and open to learn from even the most junior co-worker. Any missionary leader who gives the impression of believing that learning can only take place one-way will soon find him or herself without postmodern followers.

Related to this is the whole question of image. Boomer and Veteran missionaries look for exemplary leaders – those who look the part and can hold their own. Self-sufficiency is admired, as is the 'right' kind of dress and general behaviour 'appropriate for a Christian leader'. In direct contrast, younger missionaries are not fooled by seamless exteriors – far from it. Indeed, overly well-groomed leaders, or those who never say the wrong thing, may be suspected of covering up some big defect! Postmoderns have seen so many reliable and squeaky clean leaders (in the church as well as outside it) turn out to be frauds or abusers that they have far more confidence in a leader who acknowledges his or her failings and who makes no pretence of being better than others. At least they can identify with and make allowances for the failings of such a leader, whereas 'perfect' leaders merely have their failings well camouflaged, ready to cause havoc to the unwary. If such an assessment of leaders seems unfair, remember the frequency with which the press exposes priests who abuse children, youth leaders who seduce their 'flock', ministers who commit adultery with their secretaries, elders who beat their wives, evangelists who build personal empires by manipulating their (poor) supporters, and the myriad of apparently devoted mothers and fathers (including Christians) who secretly abuse or neglect their children.

Perhaps the key word is 'authenticity'. Xers are not fooled by exteriors. They are not fooled by claims of superior knowledge or greater spirituality. But leaders who acknowledge their weaknesses, who show themselves to be trustworthy and approachable, who prove in more than mere words that they are ready and wanting to learn from younger colleagues (whom they count as brothers and sisters in the Lord, as opposed to sons and daughters, or expendable junior soldiers), and allow themselves to be held accountable for their behaviour, can almost guarantee the loyalty, support and affection of their postmodern co-workers.

Morality

Alan and Sue Parker met each other at university and after a few
months decided to move in together to a one-bedroom apartment
just off the campus. Two years later, they both became Christians
in a mission run by the InterVarsity Christian Fellowship, a costly
decision that brought an end to their cohabitation.

A few years later, and after they had married, they had an
increasingly strong sense that God was calling them to serve him in
Argentina. During the gruelling applications process with Latin
Outreach Mission they didn't hide their sexual pasts (both had other
sexual partners prior to university) and the agency leaders made a
note in their confidential files that Alan and Sue, whilst a lovely
couple, 'carried a lot of baggage' from the past.

Soon afterwards, with the mission leadership's blessing and
assurance that their field leaders would 'look after them', they found
themselves in Buenos Aires, where they began studying Spanish in
preparation for joining a rural development team working near the
Bolivian border. Whilst Sue was a natural linguist, Alan struggled
somewhat, but both were easy-going characters and found themselves quickly befriended both by the young people at the church
they were assigned to and by their Argentinian neighbours in the
apartment block where they lived.

Before long, their neighbours started inviting them to family
celebrations and parties that usually continued into the early hours.
At first they weren't too sure whether they should go because the
alcohol tended to flow quite freely and it became clear that not all
the couples were married (at least not to each other!). But they
decided it was more important be salt and light in the world than to
risk offending their new friends, who had adopted them like a
second family. In any case, both Alan and Sue loved the noise, colour
and laughter at these events, and tried not to make comparisons with
the church they attended.

However, the leadership of both the mission and the church
began to express their concern at the Parkers' behaviour. Not only
were they present at these debauched (in the leaders' opinions) events,
but they drank beer and wine there too. It soon emerged that they
listened to rock music CDs and drank wine at home as well, both of
which were taboo for the church leaders. Moreover, the young people
at the church, knowing what Alan and Sue were doing, were

beginning to question the moral values laid down by the American missionaries who had planted the church fifteen years previously.

The field director decided it was time to talk with them and, as gently as he could, he tried to explain that their witness was being compromised by such activities and that the church leaders were very unhappy at the influence they were being on the young people. He suggested that they were slipping back to their pre-conversion sinfulness, and if they weren't very careful they would soon be affected by the lax sexual morality of their non-Christian friends, especially in view of their 'colourful' past. Alan and Sue tried to explain about wanting to be salt and light. They tried to say how they felt that the church was so culturally removed from the culture, whereas they were trying to follow Jesus' example by enjoying the company of the Argentinian equivalent of 'tax collectors and sinners', but the field director couldn't see the parallel.

Alan and Sue were left wondering what should they do – please the church or relate well to their neighbours? As for the field leader, he offered no other option than to get in line or pack their bags – not quite what they had imagined when the staff at headquarters had promised that they would be looked after.

- *Are the moral values of your church/mission determined by scripture or by evangelical subculture?*
- *To what extent can morality be contextualized or enculturated?*
- *With an increased number of potential postmodern recruits with a 'blotted' moral history and outlook, how are we going to assimilate them without marginalization?*

It is often argued that postmoderns have a much lower moral standard than previous generations. In many ways this negative understanding of postmodern morality is probably true, but we would suggest that this moral decline is not as deep or as wide as many traditionalists would have us believe. Indeed, as we shall see, in some ways postmodernity occupies the moral high ground over modernity.

In the context of mission agencies, the shift from modernity to postmodernity is resulting in a clash of moral values between postmodern missionaries and their older modernist colleagues. Younger missionaries cannot escape being moulded by post-modernism, and this moulding will include having a post-modern angle on moral issues. Indeed, the very definition of what constitutes a moral issue may be quite different, and this inevitably gives rise to tension.

It is essential that we engage missiologically and biblically with this clash of cultures if we are not to engage in cultural imperialism, with either postmodern missionaries rejecting all that their predecessors held dear, or vice versa. It is our conviction that neither world view is inherently more or less 'morally upright' than the other, any more than Maasai, Nepalese or Quechua cultures are inherently more or less moral than western European or North American cultures. However, in the context of missions, it is the older (modernist) missionary world view that holds the reins of power, and so it is the older missionaries who define what are acceptable or unacceptable moral standards, both in the missionary team and the churches they found. The result is that the younger missionary either has to change and adopt the cultural values of his or her superiors, or leave. Either way, the older cultural paradigm is perpetuated in missions agencies, postmodern missionaries continue to be an excluded minority, and the world missions movement is weaker as the insights of postmodern missionaries are lost.

At the risk of allowing modernist evangelicalism to set the agenda, we will begin by assessing perhaps the most obvious 'failing' of postmodern morality: sexual ethics. Most postmodern young people live together, or at least have sex, before marriage. In the case of homosexual relations, eventual marriage is excluded. In many cases, unmarried missionary candidates will have been sexually active prior to conversion, and indeed may be even after conversion in some cases. Married candidates may well have had an equally turbulent sexual past.

Some postmodern Christian writers have suggested that traditional sexual ethics are middle-class Anglo-Saxon values rather than being particularly Christian, and as such perhaps need to be reviewed.[4] We reject this assessment and uphold traditional

---

[4] See for example Dave Tomlinson, *The Post-Evangelical* (London: Triangle, 1995), p. 35ff.

sexual ethics as scriptural. However, where we part company with our modernist elders is on the heavy, almost exclusive, importance placed on sexual ethics whilst ignoring or even promoting other practices abhorred by the biblical writers, something we will return to shortly.

The preoccupation with sexual sin is typical of the evangelical obsession with the individual, which is itself syncretistically rooted in modernity's notion of the autonomous self, rather than scripture's self-in-community. Perhaps in reaction to liberal Christianity's emphasis on the so-called social gospel, evangelicalism has tended to focus on the salvation of individuals, and especially their souls. It is therefore not surprising that an individualistic understanding of salvation was accompanied by an individualistic understanding of discipleship and holiness, hence the evangelistic call to 'accept of Jesus as *my personal* Lord and Saviour'. Thus 'holiness' and 'morality' were reduced to personal individual sins such as sexual behaviour, dress codes, divorce, alcohol taboos, tithing, abortion, swearing, 'dirty' jokes and so on.

In contrast with modernity's obsession with the individual, postmodernity calls us back to a more holistic and community-based understanding of what it means to be human, and postmodern Christians have enthusiastically welcomed this return to scriptural values. In turn, postmodern Christians, missionaries included, are likely to be more concerned with moral issues such as weapons of mass destruction, environmental destruction, women's rights, Third World debt, racism, exploitation of child labour and so on. Major tensions are inevitable when such missionaries find themselves working alongside colleagues who wrongly attribute such concerns to worldly left-wing politics, and who themselves equate Christianity with right-wing political opinions. The tensions are heightened when in turn the post-modern missionary appears to give far less importance, or none whatsoever, to traditional evangelical virtues such as sober dress, teetotalism, the 'rightful' place of women in the home and church, and avoidance of venues such as bars and night-clubs. Indeed, many of us would argue that in some settings body piercing, drinking beer in the pub, enjoying house, indie or rock music, and wearing clothes that would upset your church elders may be part and parcel of authentic incarnational ministry in a postmodern world.

Spirituality

During the selection and training week at the sending base, Kate finally got to know a bit more about the internal workings of her chosen mission agency. It was her first real opportunity to learn, reflect, worship, pray, eat, sleep and breathe the mission. It was also a time for the agency to 'suss out' Kate to see if she was really 'mission material'.

It soon became apparent that, in what was a fairly conservative evangelical agency, Kate was somewhat out of place. Her house church background did not seem to lend itself too well to regimented styles of worshipping and praying. She also gained the strong impression that the mission's attitude to women in leadership was not what she had been led to believe.

The cut and dried instructions that were given in a seminar, 'How to keep your relationship with God healthy whilst on the field', on how to keep on track spiritually just did not match Kate's normal way of enjoying her relationship with God. Furthermore, the worship and Bible teaching sessions at the selection weekend were led only by men, despite the apparent presence of gifted women, whose ministry was limited to playing the piano or leading in prayer.

Kate had already visited the country she was destined for as a short-termer during a year off between high school and university. With the knowledge she had of the country, she knew that she would fit in well with the local church and culture there. Despite this, the selection week made her wonder whether the agency's expression of spirituality was something that she could adhere to with any integrity, or be nourished by, let alone promote in the country she would serve in.

- *Should Kate look for another route to serve in the country of her calling and look upon this as a close call?*

- Or should she sit tight, conform to the desired pattern, and hope for the best?
- What if she cannot find an agency where she feels 'at home' spiritually?

In the previous section we saw how easy it is for modern and postmodern missionaries to clash over issues of moral value judgements. But what about when their notion of the very essence of Christian spirituality collides head on? The reality is that postmodern people in general are far more spiritually aware than previous generations, and so postmodern Christian spirituality can appear quite threatening to modernist missionaries, or else very lax, depending on the way in which it is looked at. The same can be true when postmodern Christians observe the spirituality of their elders.

Traditional evangelicalism has tended to place supreme importance on one's 'personal walk with the Lord', and the church experience was designed to assist individuals achieve a closer relationship with God. Thus personal spirituality became closely linked to a daily 'quiet time'[5] (preferably held in the early morning), and church tended to focus on teaching, that is, a passing on of knowledge about God from the trained minister to the lay congregation. Spirituality was seen to be closely linked with self-discipline, particularly in terms of daily devotions and church attendance.

Postmodern Generation X Christians, including missionaries, are likely to have quite a different spirituality in a number of ways. To take a simple example of this shift, whilst many Xers still place high importance on daily personal devotions, others are not too concerned if such special times of withdrawal do not occur on a daily basis. However, both groups will consider that walking closely with the Lord throughout every day is at least as important as – if not more important than – the quiet time, be it

---

[5] However, the extent to which previous generations actually lived up to this ideal is open to debate!

daily or less frequently. Xers will seek consciously to involve God in every aspect and moment of life, at least in principle.

Furthermore, postmodern missionaries will long for an experiential angle to their spirituality. It is not sufficient to learn about God: they long to meet with God and experience his presence. As a result, they are likely to be dissatisfied, if not thoroughly bored, by traditional church services with their individualistic didactic and cerebral emphases. For them, what they long to find in church is more likely to be a community occasion, a coming together of the people of God to enjoy each others' company and the presence of God. Tea or coffee with a couple of biscuits and a superficial conversation after church is most definitely not fellowship! Indeed, the traditional evangelical focus on Sunday worship as the core church activity may be brought into question if it fails to satisfy the longing for intimate community with both God and fellow believers.

This will inevitably give rise to problems when Generation X missionaries are expected to plant churches according to a model that they themselves find boring and irrelevant. If young missionaries fail to meet with God at the church they are helping to plant, it is unlikely that they will think it worthwhile inviting their non-Christian friends. It is not uncommon to find young missionaries whose only motive for attending church is a latent sense of Christian duty, and who come away each week wondering why they bothered to go. Such a situation is acutely problematic on three levels: the personal spirituality of the younger missionary whose faith is weakened by church attendance; the ineffectiveness of the missionary as evangelist and church planter (after all, why try to draw people into a church where you rarely meet God?); and the creation of tension and division in the missionary team itself.

We suggest that it is vital that younger missionaries are released to experiment with new forms of church and worship that respond to the postmodern longing for spiritual experience, community religious expression and holistic faith. They need support and encouragement to experiment, to make mistakes and to move forwards to rediscover the meaning of church for the new cultural paradigm. Without meaning to belittle successful modernist church models, it will not do to repeat these models in a postmodern culture, for these older models were successful because they were modernist models for a modern world. But they are proving manifestly ineffective at reaching the unchurched younger postmodern generation, and cannot even retain the postmodern children of their own members. As Martin Robinson and Stuart Christine put it, 'the challenge for church planters is therefore to give birth to new forms of church rather than replicate the same structures that have already failed elsewhere'.[6] Obviously in the context of missions, the desire for a postmodern understanding of church will need to be balanced by the need to develop forms of church that are appropriate for the host culture. But we suggest that a postmodern form of church that is holistic, experiential and community focused is likely to find far greater resonance with non-Western cultures than the cerebral, individualistic and otherworldly forms of traditional evangelicalism.

In the context of spirituality, we would like also to make mention of another area of potential tension and conflict: the way in which the Bible itself is perceived and used (that is, the matter of hermeneutics). Generation X missionaries are likely to have a more moderate and provisional confidence in their own understanding of Scripture that their modernist missionary colleagues mistakenly interpret as accommodation to a liberal/postmodern rejection of absolute truth. However, it is important to stress that postmodernism doesn't so much reject the concept of absolute objective truth but rather has grave doubts about the capacity of human reason to grasp that truth. Indeed, postmodern philosophers such as Michel Foucault, Jacques Derrida and Jean-François Lyotard insist that all claims to have grasped absolute truth are in fact tools of oppression ('If I have the absolute truth, you must obey and follow me, otherwise you are deviant'). Postmodern Xer missionaries are not likely to doubt the trustworthiness and truthfulness of Scripture itself, but they will

---

[6] Martin Robinson and Stuart Christine, *Planting Tomorrow's Churches Today* (Crowborough, East Sussex: Monarch, 1992), p. 9.

probably distrust the ability of both themselves and others to interpret Scripture faultlessly. Similarly, they may well consider attempts to force particular interpretations as normative to be manipulative power tactics. They would be much more comfortable with 'provisional certainty', that is, the confident acceptance of a particular interpretation of scripture, but with the humble proviso that all our interpretations are to some extent provisional and subject to future reassessment (1 Corinthians 12:9–12). There is obviously significant potential for these divergent views of Scripture to create tension between mission agencies and older missionaries on the one hand and younger postmodern missionaries on the other.[7]

Truth and honesty

James and Rachel were busy preparing for an imminent home assignment. They had spent four years dividing their time between a small church plant and an indigenous project for street kids, and enjoyed the challenge of both ministries, especially working with the children.

The church plant had struggled numerically, and one of the church leaders had recently been diagnosed HIV positive, which had led to him confessing to visits to local prostitutes. It was evident that these visits had been suspected for a while, but because of lack of proof, the others in leadership had chosen not to challenge his behaviour.

The shelter for street kids was also having problems, and because of a series of indiscretions on the part of two of the leaders and a financial deficit, the project risked closure. James and Rachel hoped their home assignment would generate increased prayer for both projects that would result in more godly national leaders, and financial support to enable the work to continue. They were confident

---

[7] Stan Guthrie's misunderstanding and misreporting of a discussion at the Iguassu Consultation in October 1999 is a case in point. See Stan Guthrie, *Missions In The Third Millennium* (Carlisle: Paternoster, 2000), p. 163.

that their supporters in Canada (most of whom were, like them, in their mid-thirties) would pour our their hearts in intercession once they knew the harsh realities their friends were facing.

The day before they flew back to Calgary they met with their field leader for debriefing. He talked over the recent crises with them and prayed with them that God would use them to raise up more support in both prayer and giving for the projects. But as the meeting drew to a close, his tone changed, and he quietly advised them to be 'economical' with information about what was going on in the church and shelter for, as he put it, 'If the folks back home found out about some of the things that are happening here the giving may dry up.' James and Rachel found this really hard to accept. Weren't their supporters entitled to know what was being done with their money? Didn't they have to know the ugly reality if they were to pray intelligently and with passion? Wasn't it hypocritical to condemn the church leader's visits to prostitutes if the missionaries themselves were lying about the project? They put this to the leader, who smiled and told them not to be so legalistic and to 'live in the real world'.

- *Do we put at risk the integrity of our agency's ministries by not telling the whole story?*
- *To what extent are agencies driven by the need to appear successful in order to please their donors?*
- *In what other ways do mission agencies project images that do not really reflect reality?*

In view of postmodernism's scepticism about the truth, it is perhaps ironic that truthfulness, or rather the lack of truthfulness, should be one of the complaints that Generation X missionaries have against mission agencies. But on further reflection, this should not be too surprising. After all, does not postmodernism suspect truth claims simply because such claims are really a selective construction of 'truth' that favours the interests of the truth-claimer? The postmodern missionary therefore may be subconsciously questioning the previously accepted versions of truth of mission agencies, not because of a desire to undermine those agencies, but because of a concern for Christian integrity. And, despite modern evangelicalism's obsession with absolute truth, it is surprising how evangelical missions agencies are willing to be economical with the truth, albeit subconsciously. This lack of truthfulness occurs on a number of levels, and we suggest that at the root of much of this unconscious deceit (self-deceit?) is modernity's idol of success.

Mission agencies often exaggerate their results, and this can be frustrating for younger missionaries who see the other side of the story on the mission field. Mission publications lay great emphasis on conversions, but where are the stories of falling away or admissions that church growth has occurred as a result of transfer from other competing churches? One product of modernity's obsession with success and progress is that mission agencies must portray themselves as successful in order to guarantee continuing financial support from donors, but maybe the sacrifice of truth is too great a price to pay.

More importantly, mission agencies can unwittingly sell themselves to potential recruits as being very different to what they really are. Specifically, we are very concerned at the current tendency of missionary societies to work on updating their image, without the corresponding effort to ensure that this new image is reflected by the reality of life in the mission. This is particularly important in overseas locations where new recruits suddenly find themselves without the normal support structures that would enable them to cope with a similar mismatch of expectations and reality in their home countries. Any efforts to recreate the image of an agency must be accompanied by equal or greater efforts to re-educate existing missionaries, and perhaps even replace leaders who are unable to alter their attitudes.

Reducing the struggle – unity in diversity

We are very aware that most of the above makes very depressing reading, and at times it has been very depressing to write it. Yet we do not want to end here, for we believe that the task of taking the Good News of Jesus to all peoples continues to be a mandate for his church today: modern, postmodern and non-Western. We also believe that Christian disunity is a denial of the very gospel we proclaim, for 'in Christ Jesus you are all children of God through faith. As many of you as were baptized into Christ have clothed yourselves with Christ. There is no longer Jew or Greek, there is no longer slave or free, there is no longer male and female [there is no longer modern nor postmodern, there is no longer Veteran nor Boomer nor Xer nor Mosaic]; for all of you are one in Christ Jesus' (Galatians 3:26–8). This has to be our starting point and our ending point.

In many ways we are facing a situation very similar to that which Paul addressed in both the epistle to the Galatians and the epistle to the Romans. In the former, the Jewish majority in the church were seeking to impose their cultural norms on the nascent Gentile churches, and the Judaisers saw it as their God-given duty to force their Gentile brothers and sisters to obey the whole Law. Paul championed the cause of the Gentiles, and at the Council of Jerusalem (Acts 15) it was agreed that the Law given through Moses was applicable only to the Jews.

Not long afterwards, the situation in Rome was the total opposite. The Jewish believers who had been expelled from Rome by the Emperor Claudius[8] were returning to reincorporate themselves into a Gentile-majority church that had no respect for Jewish cultural traditions. Paul urged both parties to respect each others' cultural traditions, and if necessary forgo their freedom in order to avoid offending their 'weaker brethren'.

If Paul were with us now, we believe that he would be urging those of us who are committed to the missionary task to listen to one another, respect one another and learn from each other as we seek to love and serve Christ together. Like the Jewish and Gentile believers in Galatia and in Rome, the ways in which we live out

---

[8] Suetonius tells us that the Emperor Claudius 'expelled Jews from Rome because of their constant disturbances at the instigation of Chrestus' (probably a reference to the habitual disturbance that occurs in Acts whenever Jews start turning to Christ [Chrestus]), the same expulsion that caused Priscilla and Aquila to meet up with Paul in Corinth (Acts 18:2). See for example James D. G. Dunn, *Romans 1–8* (Word Biblical Commentary, vol. 38A) (Dallas, Texas: Word, 1988), pp. xliv–liv.

our discipleship, and indeed our missionary calling, may be very different depending on our cultural background. But we have a God-given obligation to respect the cultural differences between us and to free each other to serve God in ways that are appropriate to our cultures.

At times we will have to challenge each other when we use 'being faithful to our culture' as an excuse for sinning and living in syncretistic idolatry. In this chapter we have tended to focus on the failings of modernist expressions of Christianity simply because, like the Gentiles in Galatia or the Jews in Rome, we have lived for so long with the pressure from the missionary power holders to conform to the values of the alien culture that is modernity, and we long to be freed to serve God faithfully as postmodern disciples of Jesus in the emerging culture. However we are aware that without the loving and respectful fellowship of our modernist colleagues we risk a syncretism with post-modernity that is every bit as grave as evangelicalism's acceptance of modernity's value system in previous generations. But that is another topic entirely.

In view of all the above, pastoral care of younger missionaries becomes a major issue. For if the supposed providers of pastoral care and support for new missionaries (their senior colleagues) are, as a result of the clash of world views, the source and cause of major tensions and frustrations for the new worker, to whom does the Xer missionary turn to for help, support and advice when facing personal difficulties?

Our prayer is that the thoughts offered in this chapter will help the missionary movement at least to recognize and understand what is going on around us. Richard Tiplady summarizes it well when he says:

> Unity in diversity welcomes the needs and inputs of each (à la 1 Cor 12), not just despite ethnicity, gender, or generation, but because of them. We need the specific insights and perspectives of each, other-wise we are all impoverished – Gen Xers, Boomers, Veterans ... Only as we respond to, and embrace the changes in our culture, and accept

the strengths and gifts of each generation, can the church truly be a place and a messenger of reconciliation, for all generations, in a changing world.[9]

This is a message for all people across all generations, and in the context of missions it is a message that demands a radical rethink of every area of missionary theology and practice.

---

[9] Richard Tiplady 'Let X be X: Generation X and World Mission' in William D. Taylor (ed.), *Global Missiology For The 21st Century: The Iguassu Dialogue* (Grand Rapids, Michigan: Baker, 2000), pp. 474–5.

3

How to Herd Cats

Leading Generation X

Peter Stephenson

In his introduction to perhaps the best current compendium of global missiological thought, Bill Taylor suggests that 'during the last decades of the twentieth century, an unfortunate emphasis on pragmatic and reductionist thinking came to pervade the international Evangelical missionary movement', an emphasis he blames in part on lack of theological reflection and lack of attention to non-Western missiological voices.[1] I would suggest that the traditional evangelical understanding of leadership, particularly in the missionary context, has fallen victim to pragmatism and reductionism.

However, it will not do to replace one secular management paradigm with another one, regardless of how culturally appropriate it may be. As Christians, and especially as Christians committed to the missionary task of making Jesus known to the nations, we must listen intently to Scripture for, whatever richness and enlightening perspectives they may offer, cultural values are not ultimately neutral. Whatever help social sciences and management studies may offer us, we are ultimately called to

---

[1] Taylor (ed.), *Global Missiology For The 21st Century*, p. 4.

model ourselves on Jesus and the values of the Kingdom of God. It is precisely this loss of focus that has led the missionary movement to its present wilderness, and we cannot afford to repeat this mistake in the next two decades.

Many of the tensions between the missionary establishment and its representatives on the one hand and younger missions workers[2] on the other come to a head in the matter of leadership. For leaders are the ones who set the rules, the ones who define the goals, the ones who determine how those goals will be achieved. Or at least, that is the case in the modernist paradigm of leadership. But increasing numbers of younger missions workers do not subscribe to the philosophical assumptions that legitimize such an approach to leadership. Indeed, as in so many other areas, the younger workers (or potential workers) have had their approach to leaders and leadership moulded by a set of postmodern world view presuppositions that are by definition the very opposite of the modern world view of their seniors. This chapter attempts to explain the difference in attitudes to leaders and leadership, and to identify how younger missions workers (so-called Generation X and Millennials) like to be led (and consequently how they feel they are being failed by many leaders).

The postmodern attitude to leadership

Postmodernism, the dominant world view for young Western people, is extremely sceptical towards authority. Whilst in previous generations leaders were held up as folk heroes and models to follow, prominent leaders now have to fight to

---

[2] I use expressions such as older workers and younger workers as gross generalizations, and am very aware that the reality at this point in the transition from modernity to whatever comes next is vastly more complex. Furthermore, as Generation X writers, we are now approaching 40 – hardly young any more, except from the perspective of someone approaching retirement!

maintain credibility. One only needs to contrast the war movies of the sixties and seventies that my peers and I grew up with (*Battle of Britain*, *The Dambusters*, *Lawrence of Arabia*, *Patton*, *A Bridge Too Far* ...) with later military films (*Platoon*, *Gallipoli*, *A Few Good Men*, *Thirteen Days*, to name just a few) to see that leaders are now more likely to be portrayed as incompetent fools and/or dangerous manipulators than as heroes. And if the war stories ever cease to provide resources to feed suspicion of leaders, countless episodes such as Watergate, Whitewater, Enron, and (dare I say it) reflection on Operation Enduring Freedom in ten years time (to say nothing of countless cash-for-votes scandals on both sides of the Atlantic), will step in to ensure that leaders never regain unquestioning trust and respect. In the workplace too, young people quickly learn that those over them strictly keep number one's interests in first place.

Whatever the exaggerations and unfairness of the postmodern perspective (and there are many) there is more than an element of truth to these negative assessments of leaders. Even if this were not the case, the fact is that younger people, missionary personnel included, share this basic suspicion of (or at least lack of unswerving trust in) those who are over them. Older people, far from being people to look up to, are often seen as those who took an OK world and completely screwed it up before handing it on to our generation. Consider the words of a woman in her thirties concerning her boyfriend: 'He hasn't got a job – who needs one in this brave new world we are forging from the mess our parents left us.'[3]

The antagonism between leaders and young people is particularly marked between the Boomer generation and Generation X. It was the spectacular aggressively self-confident can-do attitude of the Boomers that led to economic boom in the latter part of the twentieth century. But this same boom has caused global environmental destruction, and has been paid for by exploitation of the non-Western world and the emotional suffering of a generation of children whose parents placed a higher premium

---

[3] Personal correspondence, 1998.

on their own personal freedom and success than on their offspring's need for a safe and secure family environment. And as if this were not enough, much of the Boomers' success was in their ability to harness and use the skills of their juniors. George Barna sums it up:

> Boomers sought to gain control of the decision-making apparatus from day one, intent upon redefining authority, burying tradition, and increasing their profile in business and government. The arrival of the Boomers signalled the end of predictability, the rule of fairness and the notion of the common good ... The Boomers had a single goal: to win on their own terms ... Boomers believed in the entrepreneurial way of life, but the irony is that the most successful Boomer entrepreneurs were those who cashed in on the technological breakthroughs developed by the GenXers.[4]

Douglas Coupland, as so often, puts his finger on the pulse with the story of how one of his characters, Dag, gave up his 'good' job in favour of low-pay, low-responsibility 'McJobs' that freed him to enjoy life. As Dag puts it to his Boomer boss:

> Do you really think we enjoy hearing about your brand-new million-dollar home when we can barely afford to eat Kraft Dinner sandwiches in our own grimy little shoe boxes when we're pushing thirty? A home you won in a genetic lottery, I might add, sheerly by dint of your having been born at the right time in history? You'd last about ten minutes if you were my age these days, Martin. And I have to endure pinheads like you rusting above me for the rest of my life, always grabbing the best bit of cake first and then putting a barbed-wire fence around the rest. You really make me sick.[5]

---

[4] George Barna, *Real Teens: A Contemporary Snapshot Of Youth Culture* (Ventura, California: Regal, 2001), pp. 13–14.
[5] Douglas Coupland, *Generation X* (London: Abacus, 1992), p. 26. He develops this theme further in *Microserfs* (1995). Spanish novelist Lucía Etxebarría tells a similar story in her novel *Amor, Curiosidad, Prozac y Dudas* (1997).

It should therefore come as no surprise that, having seen the damage wrought on the environment, the family and civil community, the next generation should reject all the Boomers stood for. In contrast to the Boomers, and despite their inability to create stable marriages (or, more likely, their lack of attempt to create stable marriages for fear of failure), younger people place very high importance on marriage and family. They place supreme importance on friends, human rights (including women's and gay rights) and the environment. They may not know how to achieve their longings, but they know that the Boomer way is not the road to follow.

Shouldn't Christian missionaries be different?

Boomers may rightly feel unfairly judged, especially Christian missionary Boomers who have devoted their generation's vision and entrepreneurial spirit to the task of world mission. One might also ask, shouldn't Christian young people be different? From a biblical perspective, one has to answer yes and no. On the one hand, did not the writer to the Hebrews say, 'Obey your leaders and submit to them' (Hebrews 13:17)? But on the other hand, didn't Yahweh say to Jeroboam, who later rebelled against Solomon's son, 'I am going to tear the kingdom from Solomon's hand and give ten tribes to you' (1 Kings 11:31)? Did not the Old Testament prophets consistently oppose the kings of Israel when they were unwise, unfaithful and/or unjust? Didn't Jesus himself say of the religious authorities of his day, 'Woe to you because you load people down with burdens they cannot carry, and you yourselves will not lift one finger to help them' (Luke 11:46)? One wonders whether Builder and Boomer understandings of leadership might be based more on military models (as befitting generations that grew up with two world wars and Vietnam) than on Scripture itself?

It is clear that God expects his people to respect authority, but not without conditions. It appears to us that this is precisely the attitude of most younger missions personnel. There appears to be a general initial disposition to trust and respect those placed over them in positions of authority. There is a recognition that longer-serving colleagues probably know more about mission and the host culture than the new arrival. However, it is equally clear that such respect is not unconditional, and once it has been lost it will be all but impossible to regain. Whereas previous generations may have respected authority simply because they were the ones in authority (even if they were seen to be less than perfect), for the emerging generations respect must be earned not assumed. Their trust has been betrayed too many times by national leaders, work bosses, teachers, parents, and even clergy, for it to be granted unreservedly.

It is absolutely essential for Christian leaders, and especially missions leaders, to recognize that old patterns of automatic respect for 'elders and betters' have gone, and they are not coming back again. Leaders who are foolish will no longer be given the benefit of the doubt time and again – they will soon become known as untrustworthy fools. Leaders who abuse their authority will no longer be assumed to be acting in their juniors' best interests – they will be regarded as manipulative control freaks. Leaders who use Scripture to justify their wrongful attitudes will not thereby win the argument – the junior colleague will simply add religious hypocrisy to the list of their leader's perceived failings. And mission agencies that expect junior personnel to submit unconditionally to leaders who display such characteristics will be deemed to share them. In such cases loyalty and trust have not been earned, and should not be expected. And rightly so.

Unfortunately the church, especially the evangelical wing, and even more so the missionary movement, has been extraordinarily slow to recognize this shift in a way that secular culture and business hasn't been. Perhaps this is not surprising since the church always lags behind culture, and the conservative wing from which most missionary recruits are drawn even more so. But the results on the mission fields are tragic, for again and again late-1990's scepticism meets 1950's superiority, sparks inevitably fly, and the conservative older power holders hold the trump cards, so that the younger worker is the loser, often portrayed as a rebellious trouble maker, when the reality usually couldn't be much more different.

If the new worker has had professional work experience, the difference between expectation and reality may be even more marked because the secular workplace has recognized this cultural shift and so works hard to make the young worker (on whom the success of the business depends) feel respected, listened to and valued. When I left university and began work as an engineer, I was immediately given tasks to do, and the basic assumption was that I knew what to do, and would ask for help if needed. I well remember my team leader regularly asking me, who had a fraction of his experience, for ideas of how to solve an engineering problem, and that was by no means a cutting-edge organization. Ten years later I became a missionary only to be told on arrival on the field 'Now you'll have to unlearn all they taught you at Bible College and spend the next two years learning from others.' True, this wasn't the agency's official policy (in fact, the agency's written policy was the direct opposite, which was one of the reasons I signed up!), but the impression that was clearly given by the unspoken and sometimes spoken attitudes of most old hands is that I had nothing to give and everything to learn. Frustrating to say the least! Of course new missionaries have a lot to learn – they know that. They are not idiots. Yet time and again they are treated as such.

This current situation is creating a very dangerous situation in mission agencies. Boomers came to the fore in the seventies and eighties and quickly grasped the reins of power in missions as everywhere else. In the nineties, the Xers began to appear, but there was no way the self-confident Boomers were going to quickly relinquish, or even share, power. In fact, Xers had very little interest in power – from their perspective those with power were nothing special, nor was power anything to be particularly longed for. Influence, yes. Input, yes. Respect, yes. But power? No way! Xers were and are deeply sceptical about power holders and were in no rush to seize power for themselves. Unfortunately the Boomers misread this disinterest in power as a disinterest in leadership, and so were quite happy to hold on to both leadership and power. And of course, if any Xer showed any interest in leadership, their superiors often assumed they were grasping after power! Ten years on, Xers have got fed up with being rubbished, sidelined and misunderstood, and have left the mission field in droves.

The way ahead

Whatever the future, one thing is clear: the old has gone, the new has come. Old models of leadership just will not work any longer, however wishful our thinking may be. We need to find new patterns of leadership for a new cultural context. In finishing, I would like to suggest in very broad strokes the kinds of values and principles that will characterize effective leadership in the emerging generations.

Friendship

I could have used terms like 'respect' and 'care', but Xers hate superficiality and falseness. True respect and true care will have at its core a commitment to, and a value of, the person for who he or she is, rather than simply for what he or she can contribute to the task in hand. However urgent the task may be, we are drawn back again and again to the man who, seeing urgency with an unrivalled clarity, still said to those following him: 'I have not called you servants ... I have called you friends' (John 15:15). In the management philosophy that has governed the Western missionary enterprise in recent decades, the importance of friendship has been lost. It is not that Boomers or Builders don't care – of course they do. But their focus is on the task, and people are unwittingly reduced to tools needed to carry out the task. George Barna suggests that there is a huge conceptual gap between how adults see teenagers (generally positively), and how teenagers perceive they are seen (generally negatively), and I suggest the same is true of the conceptual gap between Boomer/

Builder leadership and Generation X mission personnel. Barna
says:

> breaking down relational barriers and thereby gaining access and
> credibility will be imperatives ... [This conceptual gap] may also
> explain why so few organizations have effectively rallied young
> people around a vision ... more often than not, those organizations
> are led by adults perceived to hold negative attitudes about teens
> and young adults. Without a sense of acceptance and respect,
> young people are not prone to submitting themselves to the leader-
> ship of people or organizations that have failed to embrace them as
> people.[6]

Whilst previous generations may have been able to focus on a
task and so have a 'good working relationship' even if warmth
was absent, this is not the case for the emerging generations (or, in
the case of Xers, the emerged, greying and balding generation!).
Given the Gospel's emphasis on love, community and the church-
as-family, we see this not as a sign of emotional weakness, but as
an indication that the Holy Spirit is correcting an unbiblical
abnormality in the Western church and Western missionary
movement that non-Westerners have been conscious of for generations. Friendships take effort and, above all, time – time that for
Boomers is a commodity whose expenditure must be carefully administered. But surely, in a world marked by distrust,
community breakdown, and racial and ethnic hatred, the greatest
apologetic for the Gospel is a genuine family of faith.

Respect

This is closely related to friendship. Respect means believing the
other person has a valuable contribution to make. It means that
learning will be genuinely two-way, with the leader, however
experienced he or she is, knowing that the younger colleague has
insights the leader cannot afford to be without. The leader will

---

[6] Barna, *Real Teens*, pp. 56–7.

therefore actively seek the opinions of those under him or her, and welcome criticism not as an attack, but as an attempt to help.

Similarly, Xers need to know that the leader values their contribution to the task right from the start. However little missionary experience a new worker may have, he or she still has a richness of Christian experience as well as general life experience and, in most cases, considerable professional expertise, to offer. Indeed, arguably the newest and least culturally adapted person may be the one best able to see the glaring flaws in an existing system that all the older hands are so used to that they are considered to be normal, even normative.

Integrity

This is essential in leadership if postmoderns are to follow. Dishonestly, falseness, pretence and patronizing attitudes will very quickly erode trust and respect for a leader. Postmodern young people have been trained by Western educational methods to ask questions, to seek out the hidden agendas and hypocrisy. A leader who lacks integrity will quickly cease to be a leader even if he or she manages to hold onto the title of boss.

Openness and vulnerability

These are related to the above. A leader who counts those under his or her authority as friends will want to share problems as well as joys. That doesn't mean that the younger missionary wants to be exposed to every detail (too many Xers have had to act as marriage counsellors for their parents, when it should have been the parents helping them though adolescent crises), but rather that the veneer of 'I'm fine' is removed, failure admitted, and prayer for difficult situations is requested. If the Creator of the universe could bare his soul to his followers (Matthew 26:36ff), it is not above leaders to ask for and accept help. Care that is one-way can quickly become patronizing, and when the weaknesses and failures of the leader are all too evident, there is a crisis of integrity.

Leadership

Despite all that has been said, Xers still want leaders to lead! But
what leadership actually means in practice may be very different
to previous generations. In view of the need to respect, listen to
and learn from postmodern colleagues, the task of leaders is to
ensure that decisions are made, and to work to make sure that
those decisions are followed through. It does not mean that the
leader will be the one making the decisions, or at least not the
major ones, but rather facilitating a decision-making process in
which all the different perspectives are heard and used. This kind
of leadership is much more demanding than the authoritarian
model, for it calls for people skills and genuine respect, rather
than the simplistic application of a heavy hand. There are very
few models of this kind of leadership for the new generation
to follow, so support structures and leaders' networks will be
essential as we seek to find a way forward.

Boldness and faith

Xers have gained a reputation for wanting to be mollycoddled,
which seems rather odd for a generation that has pioneered
leaping off bridges, attached only to a piece of long rubber, as a
form of entertainment! Add to that the whole phenomenon of
MTV culture, rave music, drug taking, recreational sex and high-
risk adventure sports, and it should be clear that the last thing
that many from this globally aware, sensation-seeking generation
want is a leisurely stroll through the park. Postmoderns believe in
the supernatural, and postmodern Christians believe in a supernatural God who wants to use them to make a difference in their
lifetime. They may no longer believe in the sound bite slogans
used by previous generations to manipulate the masses, but they
want to make a difference and are prepared to be stretched by
God (but not used by other people) to do it.

4

Top Dog

Generation X as leaders

Rob Hay

The Context

As we seek to look at how Xers lead and like to be led, it is worth spending a moment to reflect on the environment they come from. They will come into mission usually from the secular workplace. A workplace that is in a post-industrial era. More and more people now live and work in the post-farm, post-factory setting. They travel. They work at home. They even work while they travel – in hotels, planes, cyber cafés, and at 'touch-down spaces'. For many people, the division between work and life is becoming blurred.[1] This does not mean they *live to work*, for indeed they very much *work to live* (a complete reversal of the boomer work ethic), but that they can multitask and would rather use 'dead time' to work than play time or family time.

The workplace is in a knowledge economy and for most of these workers the work they do is not dependent on a specific location or specific equipment (except maybe for a PC and an

---

[1] Laurence Lyons, 'Management is Dead' in *People Management Magazine*, 26 October 2000, p. 60.

Internet connection). This means that the patterns and methods of working and therefore of leading the workers has changed. Flexibility of working requires trust from managers and self-motivation from workers. The world in which most people work today is very different from that of the nine-to-five, worker–supervisor, authoritarian pyramid that shaped previous generations.

Trying to practise what you preach!

Attempting to define how Xers like to lead is something of an oxymoron. Xers are not only a generation where diversity rules, but as they are a generation still coming to terms with the effects of postmodernity itself, there is sometimes a gap between how Xers like to be led and how they lead. This is not hypocrisy. It is simply that they know how they want to be led by their own reactions, feelings and values, but figuring out how to lead in a new way that meets those needs is an ongoing work that is by no means clear for many leaders yet. I do not want to claim that we are immune to hypocrisy and will touch on some situations where I have seen this arise.

What is in no doubt is that whilst the style of Boomers was markedly different to that of the Veterans, Xer style is poles apart with very few common areas. Combine that with the radically different world of postmodernity from the modernity that shaped both Boomers and Veterans and you can see why Boomers and Xers feel they are in different galaxies, rather than just on different planets. The post-industrial workplace is a fast-moving, priority-changing, instant-results-orientated environment. It is this environment in which the postmodernity-shaped Xer is uniquely skilled to survive and thrive.

Where Xers are unable to work easily is within the old authoritarian structures with detailed planning cycles, rigid procedures and archaic systems. Xers do not make good soldiers. This means that Xers lead in ways very different from their predecessors.

Help for the future

Xers are only a taste of what is to come in the next generation – Millennials, Nexters, or whatever you call them, who have never known anything outside postmodernity and are a million light years away from Boomers and Veterans. They are just beginning to reach the missionary workforce and Xers are probably the only possible hinge between these disparate generations. To bring them successfully into mission and keep them in mission we need to provide the support structures that they need: a tall order when most Xers feel there is little yet in the way of support structures for them. However, Xers are ready and willing and see the need for this, even if, as the following statistic shows, their older colleagues do not:

> Just as they seek development for themselves, 85% are also willing (to a great or very great extent) to '*coach and develop junior colleagues*'. However, less than half say their employer expects this, reinforcing for the next generation the belief that development is not a corporate priority.[2]

Easy come, easy go

Xer leaders are learning how to lead flexibly, not just in style, but also in a revolving workforce. People come and go and that is a fact of life. It is hard for an older leader to accept but for an Xer it is part of life. Since childhood they have seen friends, parents, homes and cities come and go. Retention is possible and the Xer leader is no less concerned with retention than others, but he or she has an inbuilt acceptance that people will leave.

Today's young international high-flyers have a short career horizon and it will be difficult – but not impossible – for

---

[2] Jonathan Winter (ed.), *Riding The Wave: The New Global Career Culture Survey Highlights – Executive Summary* (Career Innovation Survey 19, Career Innovation Research Group, 1999, by Whiteway Research International).

companies to retain them. They plan to stay with their current employers for just three years, although only 8 per cent completely rule out 'staying for the long term'.

Despite their short-term career intentions, young professionals still express loyalty to their managers, clients and to their organizations. However, their greatest commitment is to their immediate colleagues and staff. This highlights the negative effects when an individual is dissatisfied and leaves.[3]

Xers like variety. They were brought up with change. Xer leaders likewise enjoy the challenge of new projects, new work and new visions. They cope with the change of personnel and have a wider view of calling and mission than many older colleagues. Seeing investments in people (such as language and orientation) as investments for the Kingdom rather than specifically for the organization is easier for Xer leaders. They see retention not so much in remaining with an individual organization for thirty years, but journeying their spiritual pilgrimage with Jesus for a lifetime, and that may mean a mix of mission and commercial work, tent making and supporting or a series of two- or three-year roles with a variety of organizations.

Today's Xer leaders have got where they are by continually training and developing themselves and therefore recognize the importance of being able to do likewise for their team. The majority of these future leaders have a strong psychological 'performance contract' with their employers, but most are searching for a 'development contract'.[4] They are looking for the ability to develop themselves and see this as at least as important as the financial rewards they can achieve. Just as they are unlikely to stay in a role where they cannot continue their development, they are unlikely to stay in a leadership role where they cannot provide development opportunities for their team, as they see themselves failing their staff in a key area. It is a bizarre but true fact that making people more employable

---

[3] Ibid.
[4] Ibid.

elsewhere will actually encourage them to stay with their present employer.[5]

Honesty, integrity, jargon and politics

Just as Xers distrust leadership they do not see as being honest and having integrity, Xer leaders try to lead in an honest and open way. They also like to be straightforward and down to earth. What their predecessors saw as management terminology showing expertise in a field, they see as business jargon that people need to use because they are insecure in their role. Contrary to the aura of magic that went with authority roles for older generations, they see leadership as just another job, something to do if you can and relinquish if you can't. If honesty is seen as a good thing it can also be a source of people problems for Xer leaders as well. They are honest, brutally honest; too honest in some situations. Telling it how it is can sometimes leave a team member feeling crushed and broken. Xer leaders need to learn more people skills and to channel their honesty rather than change it. Even in peer-to-peer transactions, what an Xer views as honest questioning dialogue, older colleagues can view as aggressive criticism. One area where Xers (be they leaders or workers) will never do as well as Boomer colleagues is in the area of corporate politics. They see it as a waste of time and just won't play the game. If the organization wants them it will have to be on their terms, for their skills; they will not jump through hoops just to fit in.

Participation or friendship

Boomers espoused participatory management (even if they struggled to practise it) but for Xer leaders the question is 'How to build and lead a team when experience has made us wary of relying on anyone at all!' We certainly won't build a team out of people thrown together with a few team-building participatory exercises and trust games like Boomers were able to do. We

[5] Ibid.

cannot do it as leaders and the team members would not do it as workers. Trust is something that is earned and work groups are often now based on friendships. With increasing singleness, break up of marriage and the increase of dysfunctional families, the workplace provides friendship and group identity more than it has done before.

Given this situation, leadership can be a puzzling role. The TV series *Friends* illustrates the kind of core identity in which Xers draw strength, love and support. What exactly is leadership in an egalitarian *Friends*-style group? Add to this the fact that Xers do not see authority as an office but as a skill or experience that gives someone the right to lead in a specific situation. Seen in this light, the leadership may shift around members of a team from time to time as the situation and needs of that situation dictate.

Hands off management and work–life balance

Boomers developed MBO (Management By Objectives) as the supervision system for their workforce. It was an attempt at non-micro management. MBO is not the style that Xer leaders are adopting. MBO was for a stable work environment where objectives were usually set for a year and performance reviewed quarterly or six monthly. Now many Xers are not even working for the same company for a year, and so Xer leaders are developing MBP (Management By Project), recognizing that Xers often work on a project for less than a year, and usually work on multiple but diverse projects at the same time.

Another area in which Xers are demanding greater freedom than any previous generation is that of work–life balance. Achieving work–life balance is one of the greatest challenges Xers face. Almost all (94 per cent) are willing to work long hours to some extent, but nearly one-fifth of these men and women would like to work part-time and 41 per cent would like more choice over working hours.[6] Xer leaders understand the desire for work–life balance and seek to ensure their staff have a sensible and

---

[6] Ibid.

healthy balance between work, family and recreation. After all they were the generation that saw children, families and marriages sacrificed on the altar of work! For them, twelve-hour days and seven-day weeks either means bad management, or that the organization is too cheap to get enough staff to do the job!

Leadership is no longer a lonely role

It was always said that the role of the leader was a lonely one. That is now no longer necessarily the case. Just as Xer leaders are willing and able to relinquish the mantle of leadership if a better leader comes along, they are also able to share the frustrations, challenges and needs of their leadership role with others. Executive coaching is one of the fastest growing business areas and the emergence of peer support groups for CEOs is testament to this fact.[7]

Leadership of people who have been taught to have diverse viewpoints by someone who was taught to discuss, and to debate but not dictate those viewpoints, can be a challenge. Combine this with the Xers' need to value and support the values and vision of their work (rather than the Boomer approach of justifying the means with the large cheque at the end) and we can see why leaders need support for solving problems and issues in an increasingly complex workforce.

Hope for the future

Much of what we have described about Xer leadership styles is taken from the corporate or at least non-mission world, but as we

---

[7] CEOs are paying up to £8,000 per year for membership of peer support groups. For further information on this area see Widget Finn, 'Someone to Lean On' in *Director Magazine*, Institute of Directors, February 2002, p. 42. An example in a mission context is the recent responses to CEO events organized by Global Connections and the Oxford Centre for Mission Studies and plans for an informal forum explicitly for open sharing and support.

have said, it is the world from which Xers missionaries come and
therefore we need to understand it to realize that it is usually a
very different world from that of the mission agencies. Mission
agencies are usually some years behind secular changes, but an
unwillingness to examine the 'real world' and apply that knowledge to the missions world will undoubtedly inhibit missions'
ability to recruit and retain both leaders and workers from the
Xer age group. We need to change because there is too much
potential to miss out on. Some other findings from recent reports
highlight the huge potential this generation has for the work of
Jesus' Great Commission:

- At the bottom of the list of 'career values' is stability. Instead,
  high-flyers rely more on their employability – their ability to
  keep options open and maximize their personal and professional development – to ensure future success.
- Over two-thirds (69 per cent) say that an international work
  assignment is important for their personal development; 36 per
  cent would be willing to live and work abroad for more than
  five years; and, surprisingly, almost half of those with a partner
  (48 per cent) or with children (46 per cent) report their mobility
  is not constrained.
- Their top three 'career values' are wide horizons, work–life
  balance and professional expertise. (Wide horizons refers to
  maximizing future options, meeting new people, and having
  new and different experiences.)[8]

Lip service or the fruits of frustration?

I mentioned at the start that Xers are not immune to hypocrisy in
the area of leading. I have seen this arise several times, with Xers
who have been working within an organization for some time
and who may have been waiting for an opportunity to move into
a leadership position and change the systems and structures that
they and their fellow Xer colleagues find stifling, frustrating and

---

[8] Winter (ed.), *Riding The Wave*.

demotivating. However, in these situations the current leaders (and therefore the gatekeepers to the potential leadership roles) are usually predominantly Boomer or Veteran who do not see the Xers fitting in with the existing system and style. Whether spoken or unspoken, there seems to come a time for some Xers when they finally decide, consciously or unconsciously, to conform to the system in an effort to be acceptable and appointable. Often they tell themselves that once they are in position they will be true to themselves, but the reality is that usually they become pseudo-boomers adopting and utilizing the very styles and practices they found so abhorrent in their leaders!

Summing up

When we look at Xers and in particular Xer leaders and wonder why they are struggling to know how to lead their own generation, it should be remembered that innovative Boomer leaders were described as ones who could 'think outside of the box'. It has been said that Xers (workers and leaders) don't need to think outside of the box because they live outside of the box![9] Outside of the box is a brave new world, and not only are leaders still trying to discover the rules, they are discovering that the rules they have managed to find are flexible, changeable and almost certainly cannot be applied unilaterally to this diverse and disparate workforce.

---

[9] Eila Rana, 'Generation Y: The Rules of Attraction' in *People Management Magazine*, 12 July 2001, p. 10.

Part 2

The end of the world as we know it
(That says it all, really)

5

Postmodernism is not the Antichrist

Paula Harris

Somebody thinks it is? Why is that? Oh, because it's such a huge shift, and anything so different must be evil. That's what we said at the Reformation, and the Industrial Revolution, isn't it?

My friend Becky

I saw a story on CNN about a scientific evaluation of an herb. The reporter gave the story: the new study demonstrated that the herb, St John's wort, did not relieve depression, whereas thirty previous studies had said that it did. Afterwards, Lynn Russell, the anchorwoman, asked, 'Who funded the study?' Well, it was Pfizer (a major drug company). 'Don't they make Zoloft?', Russell responded. Yes, they do. Zoloft is a major anti-depressant drug. As the story continued it was reported that Pfizer used to sell St John's wort, but they stopped a year ago because it wasn't making any money. End of story. Now, I didn't watch the news in the fifties, but I assume it wasn't like this. I find both the reporter's information as well as Russell's questions helpful in determining the 'true story' about this scientific study on St John's wort. But Russell's questions are an example of postmodern culture at work. What's your response to the story? Maybe you like it, to see postmodern questions deconstructing Pfizer's 'story' that the chemicals they make are *de facto* more effective than herbs. Maybe you like the rigorous scientific pursuit of 'truth' about

St John's wort. Maybe you don't like it for some reasons of your own.

Postmodernism is like that. Its questions make things seem more complicated than we thought they were, as it tries to stop us from telling one-sided stories that manipulate and dominate other aspects of the truth. But postmodernism does not confront Jesus and the Gospel: it confronts and undermines modern culture and the ideas modernity was based upon. 'The only agreed upon element', says J. I. Packer, 'is that postmodernism is a negation of modernism.'[1] As Christians involved in mission, this should not worry us, because, hey, we believe that God works through cultural forces. God is not frightened by postmodernity. Perhaps God will even use postmodernity to undermine the syncretism of the Western church with modern culture. We owe our allegiance and worship to Jesus alone. Why should we defend the idols of modernity? Modernity had a culture and it was good and appropriate for Christians of the modern era to seek ways in which the Gospel could be culturally expressed. It was helpful for Christians to seek the Gospel's answers to the questions of modernity. But now we must acknowledge that postmodernity also has a culture. As Christian missionaries in a postmodern world, we should not react defensively to postmodernity but watch, listen, inquire and learn … common skills of any missionary. Living as followers of Jesus among postmodern people who have rejected modernity, they might help us see the idols of modernity. They might give insight into places where our churches and mission work have become captive to modernity. They might even point out syncretism in our faith, which we must reject as we preach Jesus and his Gospel. Finally, as good missionaries, we must be prepared to discern, understand and affirm what God is already doing in postmodern culture as we live in faithful hope that the Holy Spirit is at work.

---

[1] J. I. Packer quoted in David Goetz, 'The Riddle of Our Postmodern Culture: What is Postmodernism? Should We Even Care?' in *Leadership Journal* (Winter 1997) (see web sites <ChristianityToday.com>, <LeadershipJounal.net>).

How many stories?

Let's start at the beginning. Just what is postmodernism and what does postmodern mean? One of the first people to begin to define and try to understand postmodernism was Jean-François Lyotard, who published the seminal book *The Postmodern Condition* in 1979.[2] This book set out to survey the status of scientific and technological knowledge and ended up in the domain of epistemology. Lyotard became interested in the question of how science legitimizes itself, makes itself believable, or writes its own history. In accounting for how postmodernity began, Lyotard looked at the Holocaust. He described Auschwitz as 'a crime opening postmodernity' because it fully expressed modernity's goal of 'the realization of universality' and morally destroyed modernity's goal by 'liquidating it'.[3] Zygmunt Bauman takes this same line, arguing that the modern idolization of reason and pragmatism are important indirect causes of genocide. The values of efficiency, cost–benefit analysis and functionalism made mass killing possible.[4] Taking this view of the effects of knowledge, Lyotard defined postmodernism as 'incredulity towards metanarratives'.[5]

His term 'metanarratives' can be roughly explained as universal guiding principles, systems of thought, grand stories that control, contain and interpret reality.[6] They claim to be able to account for and explain all other, lesser, stories. It's easy enough to recognize a metanarrative – they are defended by force,

---

[2] Jean-François Lyotard, *The Postmodern Condition: A Report On Knowledge*, Geoff Bennington and Brian Massumi (trs) (London: Methuen, 1984).

[3] Jean-François Lyotard, *The Postmodern Explained To Children: Correspondence 1982–1985* (London: Turnaround Press, 1992).

[4] Zygmunt Bauman, *Modernity And The Holocaust* (Cambridge: Polity Press, 1989).

[5] Lyotard, *The Postmodern Condition*, p. xxvi.

[6] Steven Conner, *Postmodernist Culture: An Introduction To Theories Of The Contemporary* (Oxford and Cambridge, Massachusetts: Blackwell, 1997).

perpetuate violence, and are instruments of power. They ignore and obscure other local narratives, other versions of the truth. So postmodernity's incredulity functions to undermine and critique the 'grand story'/theory of reality that props up a false power structure. In other words, by asking questions, the postmodern opens up multiple stories. Postmodernity undermines meta-narratives by exploring and listening to local narratives, other voices that have been marginalized or other understandings of reality.[7]

Is there one history? One narrative? We've all studied 'history' in school. In Texas state schools I studied the history of brave English pioneers settling the empty west. My own Texan grand-father came from a Welsh–Irish immigrant family, after a few generations in Virginia, so this rang true to me. Yes, they were brave. Yes, Texas did (and does) have a lot of empty land. I never wondered about the stories of my Mexican schoolmates, or the Native Americans who were largely missing from Texas even then. Years later in grad school, I went to Mexico with a housemate, who was from Spain. Wandering through a museum in Juarez, we read about the brave Latinos who were brutalized by the Spanish conquistadores and forced south by the cowardly Anglos. Ah. Now what? During the Rwandan genocide, our American(?!) genocide of Native Americans began sinking home in my heart. To understand those massacres I began to read about mine. Which history is true? All of them? None?

The more we encounter people of cultures other than our own, the more we realize we are truly different. In the year 2002, it would be absurd to say there is one history of the world. What about our ideals and values? What do abstract words such as 'courage' and 'cowardice' mean? The firefighters of New York who cleaned up after the World Trade Center attacks were clearly courageous. From this side of the Atlantic, suicide bombers are cowardly. On the other hand, it takes some courage to lay your life down in the cause of your mission. So whether these men are 'courageous' or 'cowardly' depends on the history and cultural

---

[7] Lyotard, *The Postmodern Condition*.

context of the person making the judgement. Responding to the 11 September attacks from a postmodern perspective, scholar Stanley Fish wrote in the *New York Times*:

> Invoking the abstract notions of justice and truth to support our cause wouldn't be effective anyway because our adversaries lay claim to the same language. (No one declares himself to be an apostle of injustice.) ... But of course it's not really postmodernism that people are bothered by. It's the idea that our adversaries have emerged not from some primordial darkness, but from a history that has equipped them with reasons and motives and even with a perverted version of some virtues.[8]

The worldview clash we experience in a multicultural world forces us to realize there are many local histories. Here in the States, any good university and many high schools will offer courses in Western history, Asian history, African history, women's history, and others. These courses may teach contradictory versions of events and 'facts', which are impossible to integrate into a cohesive picture of the world. We have all learned the truism that the winner writes history. So, the bombings of Hiroshima and Nagasaki are described as simply the final stages of World War II, instead of acts of terrorism, or experiments with a new bomb. Anyone outside of a power structure (the 'loser') has learnt the converse. Nietzsche describes it like this: the human will to truth is often a distortion (through social and psychological factors) of the will to power. So, for example, Pfizer sponsors a study debunking the adequacy of St John's wort as they decide to stop selling it because it is not helping the company economically. On the face of things, this is expressed as a concern for the purity of truth, but actually it is an expression of malice and hate, says Nietzsche. In other words, history is written by the powerful, to maintain their power.

The postmodern context is raising new questions for modern missions. Postmodern scholars frequently describe Christianity

---

[8] Stanley Fish, 'Condemnation without Absolutes' in the *New York Times*, 15 October 2001.

as a metanarrative that is attempting to define and dominate other local narratives. Our doctrines of mission, such as 'the salvation of all nations', are also metanarratives. We claim to explain all other religions. To be relevant today, our apologetics must respond to the accurate critique that we have provided the metanarratives for slavery, for women's oppression, for apartheid, for the Holocaust ('Jews killed Jesus'), for the Native American boarding school movement[9] and the cultural genocide of indigenous peoples around the world. I could go on and on. I haven't even mentioned the Crusades. Postmodern seekers of God seriously wonder how Christian 'truth' can result in such cruelty and I believe Jesus will answer them. We Christians in a postmodern context must ask ourselves, 'Am I holding my understanding of the Gospel with humility?' and 'Does my faith express itself in gentleness, kindness and a concern for justice?'

How do we define and describe our faith? What is its evidence? Take, for example, the matter of morality and immorality. In Acts 10–15, the early church found itself in a culturally shifting situation as more people accepted Jesus. Suddenly the Christians were no longer all Jews, but there were Gentile Christians, with their own cultural context. So who defines what is moral? Is morality separate from life? From story and history? In a book with the ominous title *Truth or Consequences: The Promise and Perils of Postmodernism*, Millard Erickson writes about morality in the modern era. Morality was a 'distinct and autonomous domain ... primarily a matter of rules ... [and] these rules were negative prohibitions'.[10] Oh yes, any of us who were raised in a

---

[9] For several generations in the Americas, Christian (Anglican, Catholic, Evangelical) missionaries took children from Native American parents and extended families, enrolled them in boarding schools, and punished them if they spoke their own language or expressed their tribal culture. This was intended to be a positive expression of Christian mission. See, for example, Basil H. Johnston, *Indian School Days* (Norman, Oklahoma: University of Oklahoma Press, 1989).

[10] Millard Erickson, *Truth Or Consequences: The Promise And Perils Of Postmodernism* (Downers Grove, Illinois: IVP, 2001), p. 24.

Christian home and church would recognize this. Perhaps you have a mental rule list of what is 'immoral'. When I was thirteen, I went with my youth group from Texas to Mexico for a mission trip. On a night off, I was invited by my Mexican host family to attend a cockfight. So I went. When I returned, my youth pastor confronted me and almost sent me home from the mission trip. Cockfights were immoral. I still do not know if he was concerned about the gambling, my staying out late, the violence against the roosters, or something else I failed to notice. It could be there are cultural issues in Texas that I did not understand. He was too angry to say, and I was too puzzled to ask. When he called my parents, they explained cultural differences to me and told me to submit to him, as my authority. I apologized. I was not sent home from the mission trip. I did not attend future cockfights.

In his book on postmodernism, Erickson writes of modern moral frameworks that 'a strong sense of impropriety was attached to violations of customs, and this impropriety was thought of as immorality'.[11] Our era is truly a multicultural one. As Christians in mission, we cannot afford a simplistic 'morality' that is primarily a list of negative offenses defined by our own culture. It is an obstacle to the Gospel if we cannot see past nose rings and tattoos to a person's spiritual journey and how his or her spirituality and morality are truly and tangibly expressed in his or her life. In Acts, Peter (after his vision!) stands up to the Jerusalem council and says, basically, that God gave the Gentiles the Gospel: 'Now therefore why are you putting God to the test by placing on the neck of the disciples a yoke that neither our ancestors nor we have been able to bear?' (Acts 15:10). Then the Jerusalem leaders agree, and give four simple prohibitions: 'we should not trouble those Gentiles who are turning to God, but we should write to them to abstain only from things polluted by idols and from fornication and from whatever has been strangled and from blood' (Acts 15:19–20).

This is a very interesting list. As contemporary Christians, whether modern or postmodern, I would venture only items one

---

[11] Ibid.

(stay away from the idols of our culture) and two (avoid fornication) would still be important to us. How many of us keep kosher regulations with regards to meat? But items three and four may have stood in the way of healthy intercultural relationships between Jewish and Gentile Christians.

I grew up in the church with a very well-defined sense of 'morality' and this has become an obstacle to me in Christian mission. I remember that the first time I saw a friend smoking, it deeply offended my sense of Christian 'morality'. Gradually, I gave myself permission to wonder, what is religion? What is moral? When I could honestly ask, I could learn. 'He has told you, O mortal, what is good; and what does the Lord require of you but to do justice, and to love kindness, and to walk humbly with your God?' (Micah 6:8). Ah, in that case, my whole church was immoral and the smoking was of far less consequence. Do justice. Love kindness. Walk humbly. It's put even more strongly in Isaiah, where God says to his worshippers, Stop trampling my courts, your services are a burden to me, I will not hear your prayers because your hands are full of blood. Cleanse yourself! (summary of Isaiah 1:11–20). 'Learn to do good; seek justice, rescue the oppressed, defend the orphan, plead for the widow' (Isaiah 1:17). Those initial questions 'What is religion?' 'What is moral?' 'What is good?' were profoundly important for me in my growing spiritual journey. God has used postmodernism to ask questions of the modern religion I inherited. I have learned from postmodernism that I do not have all the answers.

What does postmodernism do?

What is postmodernism? Another stream of postmodernism is found in the arts and artistic culture. I divide it from the other disciplines like science and history because this stream ironically uses, undermines and interacts with the modern languages of art, literature and image. This stream has been characterized as a 'culture of interruptions', where forms from different cultures and disciplines combine and create new things that draw on other histories (not their own). In this stream, ideas move analogically and not genealogically. They multiply; they do not progress. Dialogue of scholars in an artistic discipline does not keep to a single field. Instead there is a rapid interchange of ideas between many disciplines and interpretive reflections are applied from one to another discipline. Literary critic Stanley Fish says we should not ask 'what does postmodernism mean?' but 'what does postmodernism *do*'.[12] In other words, how does it function?

Postmodern critical theories such as deconstruction and post-structuralism reject ideas of representation and authorial intention (in other words, that we can know what the author meant) and help us acknowledge the failure of language to completely master, control or contain truth, or the idea that truth can be transferred from one person (writer) to another (reader). Poststucturalism describes the way we attempt to pin down ideas using words, but the words are never completely accurate. The ideas slip out from under our words and we must continually use new words to attempt to pin them down and convey our message. So for example, there is a person, and I describe that person as 'Indian', but he says, 'No, I am not from India, this is my land,' so I use the words 'Native American' to describe him. And he responds, 'No, I was here before you were, and before it was America.' So I say OK, and call him an 'indigenous' person or 'aboriginal' person from the 'First Nations', at which point people in my church that I'm talking to have no idea who I am talking about. Maybe older people in his community also have no idea that they are no longer 'Indians': they are now 'First Nations'. You see how ideas slip out from under our words.

Or take the recipients of Christian mission. Luther called them 'erring pagans'. My grandparents too, might have used such language. (Missionaries must correct their errors!) My parents would have said 'the lost'. (Missionaries must save them! Or no, that can't be right. Missionaries must help them find God, who

---

[12] Stanley Fish, *Is There A Text In This Class? The Authority Of Interpretive Communities* (Cambridge, Massachusetts: Harvard University Press, 1980).

will save them.) So now the Baby-Boomers at Willow Creek[13] call these people 'seekers'. (Missionaries must find them? No. Help them be found?) Oh dear. Who are these people who receive mission again? What is it that missionaries must do?

Another aspect of postmodern thinking that is relevant here is the idea of *différance*. I will not attempt to define *différance*, because any attempt to define it pretty much misses the point. *Différance* is a way of thinking or reading which concerns itself with decentering a text or idea. In the most famous example, the French scholar Michel Foucault tells a story from Jorge Luis Borges (the Latin American novelist). In this story Borges quoted a Chinese encyclopaedia cataloguing the Emperor's animals: pigs, dead animals, tame animals, birds, stray dogs, painted animals, etc. It seems to me a very random list. Foucault wrote that the encyclopaedia list 'controlled' the animals, reinforcing the Emperor's ownership of the animals, and he argued that the encyclopaedia is disturbing and monstrous because it does not allow any ordering principle other than its own.[14] But the interesting and very postmodern thing is, once the list has been quoted and requoted, the act of repeating it and framing it undermines its power. So, when I inserted my opinion about the randomness of the list, the idea that controlled has been limited and reinterpreted. This is how postmodernity functions.

Similarly, my ironic repeating of actual names for non-Christians, within the context of poststructuralist criticism, has served to reframe and limit the power of those categories or names. When I say 'pagans' become 'lost' become 'seekers', it puts the questions somewhere in your mind: 'Who decided on those names?' 'But what if they're not?' 'What if they're just Muslim or Jewish or atheist and not looking for Jesus?' Or maybe, 'What would the non-Christians themselves think of those labels?' Or perhaps you ask, 'If the categories change that much, what is the reality being described? How arbitrary is

---

[13] A large and growing church and church network in the USA.
[14] Michel Foucault, *The Order Of Things: An Archeology Of The Human Sciences* (London: Tavistock Press, 1970).

the reality described by those three terms?' No matter which questions you ask, we find ourselves looking for new names for the people who receive Christian mission. Or it is possible that you simply ask, 'Why is she mocking well-meant missionary categories for lost seekers? That language was appropriate for that time in history.' In other words, if you don't agree with my metanarrative about postmodernity, you want to ask instead, 'How dare she use her power as an author to make me ask questions I don't agree with?' Either way, postmodern thinking is functioning. This is also how postmodernity became expressed culturally. The cultural expression reveals the assumptions of ordinary Western, or Western-educated people. The language of the postmodern academic may be almost incoherent. Many people aren't familiar with the vocabulary and they certainly don't go around talking about postmodernity, but the ideas and values are everywhere in our Western cultures.

Back to the Drugs

Let's go back to the Pfizer study of St John's wort, which sits at an interesting intersection of postmodern culture, science and the news (or public stories). Some of the questions postmodern culture teaches us to ask are:

- Who's telling the story? (Even science has stories – the story of the St John's wort study was 'Take drugs, not herbs. Herbs don't really work.')
- How does the story prop up their power?
- How do they know? Who did they ask?
- Who's not talking? Which stories are not being told?
- What do they want me to buy/do (i.e. how are they controlling or manipulating me with this story)?

I find these are helpful questions, as are the many others that follow when I ask them. As a Christian believer, I find God is good enough, loving enough and powerful enough to allow my questions. I have learnt that my faith is resilient enough for me to pose them, trusting in God's goodness and steadfast love. I have learnt that it is good for my soul to say, 'I do not know,' to ask God, and to seek the answer in God's word. Even then, sometimes I am left not knowing, or 'knowing through a glass darkly', as St Paul puts it in 1 Corinthians.

At the same time, postmodern culture is characterized by an intense commitment to pluralism (maybe that makes you nervous). Before you mentally defend against the 'slippery slope' of pluralism, I suppose that most contemporary missionaries living in the Middle East would be somewhat in favor of pluralism, perhaps especially religious pluralism. Don't you think also that the values and stories of the Gospel, the lives of Christians, would have a beautiful witness if given a chance in an Islamic culture? The early church didn't seem frightened of pluralism, nor did missionaries in Scripture. Look at Paul in Acts 17. It's only in a post-Constantinian world that we feel it's frightening. Being a Christian in a pluralistic context is hard work. We would have to win our way. Perhaps we have become used to being the dominant religion in the West, allied with political, military and economic power.

In 'The Culture of Modernity as a Missionary Challenge' Wilbert Shenk writes, 'the church is most at risk when it has been present in a culture for a long period so that it no longer conceives of its relation to culture in terms of missionary encounter'.[15] Missiologist Mary Mott is more direct, writing of the modern church, 'from a missionary perspective, Christians in the United States are perhaps in a situation where the Gospel has been so adapted to the cultural–societal demands that it no longer raises any questions'.[16] James Engel and William Dyrness say, 'Western missions theology and practice has fallen captive to modernity – a pattern of thinking that has been especially prevalent in America

---

[15] Charles Van Engen, Dean S. Gilliland and Paul Pierson (eds), *The Good News Of The Kingdom: Mission Theology For The Third Millenium* (Maryknoll, New York: Orbis, 1997).

[16] Mary Mott in ibid. p. 124.

for almost two hundred years.'[17] They go on to describe the fruit of that captivity:

> ... An outlook that envisions world missions as a movement from a political and economic power center outward toward a poor and needy periphery, which is viewed as 'the mission field' ... religious belief has come to be perceived as little more than a private and personal affair in isolation from the larger political and social world ... the Western missionary outlook and practice has become infused with rationalism – a pattern of pragmatic and managerially motivated reasoning through which methods and techniques have come to drive both mission theology and strategy in many circles.[18]

As I said at the beginning, postmodernity is not about deconstructing the Gospel. It is about deconstructing modernity. Far from being frightened of postmodernity, we should welcome its questions – they will help us seek ways to enculturate the Gospel for a new generation. Postmodernity does not confront Jesus; it confronts the idols of modern culture that we in the West have failed to renounce. With the words of wisdom from the elders in Acts 15, we now know that no culture can retain its tribal deities when we become Christian. Theologian and cross-cultural scholar Miroslav Volf says the shift from modern to postmodern culture is helping us to identify our tribal idols in the West. He identifies our idols as belief in human progress, reason, technology, quantification and the attempt to build a heaven out of worldly hell.[19] Missiologist David Bosch makes a similar list for what happened to the church and mission under modernity:

---

[17] James Engel and William Dyrness, *Changing The Mind Of Missions: Where Have We Gone Wrong?* (Downers Grove, Illinois: IVP, 2000).
[18] Ibid. p. 174.
[19] Miroslav Volf, *Exclusion And Embrace: A Theological Exploration Of Identity, Otherness And Reconciliation* (Nashville, Tennessee: Abingdon Press, 1996).

- Reason supplanted faith as a beginning point for Christians and missionaries. A fact/value distinction was created and applied to science/religion. Christians responded by desperately defending the 'objective truth' (e.g. 'fact' of religion).
- The Enlightenment's strict subject–object separation was applied to theology ... creating an 'ugly ditch' of history separating us from the past.
- The church and mission became captive to the philosophy of progress ... 'the idea of the imminent this-worldly global triumph of Christianity ... is intimately related to the modern spirit'.
- Christians came to believe the idea that all problems were in principle solvable, ruling out miracles, pushing God to the margins of human knowledge and ingenuity, and attempting to ignore or resolve the problem of evil.
- The church disintegrated into a loose gathering of 'emancipated, autonomous individuals' who made their own decisions about what they believed.[20]

Richard Rohr describes the same phenomena with different language, saying that postmodernism helps us rediscover mystery as we question whether modern objectivity was possible or even real.[21] Wait, we ask, if we don't have objectivity, aren't we floating around in subjectivism? Rohr responds that postmodernism removed the idea that the opposite of subjectivism is objectivity – and replaces it with 'the other'. In other words, the only way humans can overcome our subjectivism is in dialogue with God and with people who are different from us. Through our dialogue, and in our listening to those unlike ourselves, and to God, we may approach a better understanding of what is true.

---

[20] David Bosch, *Transforming Mission: Paradigm Shifts In Theology Of Mission* (Maryknoll, New York: Orbis, 1997), pp. 269–72.
[21] Richard Rohr, *Job And The Mystery Of Suffering* (Leominster, UK: Gracewing, 1997).

An InterVarsity USA[22] group studying student culture recently drew up a cultural taxonomy between modern and postmodern culture. They identified four shifts:

- From objective to subjective.
- From autonomous individual to community.
- From the metanarrative of progress to micronarratives.
- From word to image.[23]

If this is an accurate taxonomy, and my colleagues on campus think it is, postmodern culture will not place much value on a modern church and mission, unless it is expressed in a community of believers who acknowledge their subjectivity, whose work empowers many perspectives, and which uses visual media.

In this modern–postmodern shift, let us seek wisdom from Paul, who advised the church during its Jewish–Gentile tension. Let us all be like missionaries, and say with Paul:

> For though I am free with respect to all, I have made myself a slave to all, so that I might win more of them. 20 To the Jews I became as a Jew, in order to win Jews. To those under the law I became as one under the law (though I myself am not under the law) so that I might win those under the law. 21 To those outside the law I became as one outside the law (though I am not free from God's law but am under Christ's law) so that I might win those outside the law. 22 To the weak I became weak, so that I might win the weak. I have become all things to all people, that I might by all means save some (1 Corinthians 9:19–22).

---

[22] InterVarsity Christian Fellowship USA and the Universities and Colleges Christian Fellowship in Great Britain are both member movements of the International Fellowship of Evangelical Students, a locally led movement of Christian students in over 140 countries.

[23] Emerging Culture project as quoted in *Reaching The Coming Generations: Leading Edge Courses To Sharpen Your Church* (Madison, Wisconsin: InterVarsity Christian Fellowship, 2000), 5:3.

To the rest – to Christians who are coming from postmodern culture – I say with St Paul, 'Let each of you lead the life that the Lord has assigned, to which God called you. This is my rule in all the churches ...' Don't worry about outward forms of religion, he says, but 'remain in the condition in which you were called'. If you were a slave, then don't worry about it. Serve God with your present condition. If you were free, you're now God's slave. 'You were bought with a price, do not become slaves of human masters. In whatever condition you were called, brothers and sisters, there remain with God' (1 Corinthians 7:17–24). When we enter postmodern culture as missionaries and when we stay there as faithful followers of Jesus Christ, we will be able to discern where the Gospel deeply answers postmodern questions. Eventually, we will ask, 'What are the idols of postmodernity?' – but that is beyond the scope of this brief chapter.

6

Is a 'postmodern organization' an oxymoron?

Postmodern thought and organizational structure

Richard Tiplady

One of the main theses of this book is that postmodern thought is not the threat to all things good, holy and true that it is sometimes, rather shrilly, claimed to be. One area where Christians can learn from listening to postmodern writers is in their critique of power. Jean-François Lyotard's now famous definition of postmodernity as 'incredulity towards metanarratives' was based upon his observation that all metanarratives (big, all-embracing systems of thought) have been used in the past not to promote human freedom, but to control, to exclude, and to marginalize. If we really believe that the Gospel is 'good news for the poor', and take seriously Jesus' own decision to fraternize with prostitutes, collaborators and sundry other 'sinners' rather than with the respectable, law-abiding, God-fearing citizens of his day, then we can take the postmodern critique of metanarratives seriously and use it as a way to help us follow Jesus Christ in today's world.

It is, of course, one thing to critique, and another thing entirely to offer coherent or viable alternatives. For example, the variety of groups that make up the anti-economic globalization movement all have valid things to say about the shortcomings of the emerging global economic structures. Books such as Naomi Klein's *No Logo*, George Monbiot's *Captive State* and Noreena Hertz's *The Silent Takeover* all show us how neo-liberal economic globalization does not act as 'a rising tide to lift all boats', as its advocates assume or claim, but in fact only creates a 'level playing field' wherein the stronger nations of the world can more efficiently and effectively exploit the weak. But sadly none of these writers really offers us a viable alternative. Similarly, postmodernity can often be characterized by what it is not rather than by what it is. There is a sense that we may not yet know what will succeed high modernity and that we are in a transition phase. During this time of transition, all sorts of ideas and ways of looking at the world come crawling out of the woodwork, clamouring to become the next metanarrative that will shape our outlook and world view.

In addition to this, organizations that have been described as 'postmodern' in recent years have not necessarily had happy endings. Enron, and lesser corporations such as Global Crossing, Tyco and Telemonde, all recently collapsed or came close to doing so. They didn't bother themselves with nasty, complicated activities like actually producing anything. They concentrated on trading and derivatives, buying and selling intangibles such as the right to claim gas supply, bandwidth and the like. No heavy modernistic structures would slow these organizations down in their quest to be flexible and able to respond to new market conditions almost overnight. Describing Telemonde, journalist Jamie Doward wrote that 'it opted for a suitably sexy postmodern business model, eschewing the idea of owning assets in preference for a "weightless" approach, in which it leased capacity from some firms and sold it on to others, effectively acting as a broker of bandwidth. And, naturally, it is now on the brink of bankruptcy'.[1] Enron, of course, was even more postmodern in that it didn't allow troublesome concepts like truth or reality to confuse its accounting practices and reporting.

---

[1] Business and Media section of *The Observer*, 17 February 2002.

Having started thus, noting how postmodernity isn't necessarily a coherent concept and noting the failure of some 'postmodern' corporations, you might be forgiven for wondering if there is anything good that can be drawn from postmodern thought and applied to the way mission agencies are structured and operate. Of course, if I really thought that there wasn't, this would be a very short chapter.

The social reality of new organizational structures

It will be useful at this point to draw a distinction between the concepts of 'postmodernity' and 'postmodernism'. By the former, I mean the social and cultural changes that are perceived to be impacting the world at this point in history. Management guru Peter Drucker wrote:

> Every few hundred years in Western history there occurs a sharp transformation ... within a few short decades, society rearranges itself – its worldview, its basic values, its social and political structure, its arts, its key institutions. Fifty years later, there is a new world. And the people born then cannot even imagine the world in which their grandparents lived, and into which their own parents were born. We are currently living through just such a transformation.[2]

It is the assumption of those of us involved in the Holy Island Roundtable, and in the writing of this book, that the phenomena we describe as 'postmodernity' are evidence of just such a change happening at the moment. Part of the tension we are currently experiencing, and the reason that postmodernity can sometimes be more easily described by what it is not rather than what it is, is, as Drucker noted, that it takes 'a few decades' to work through. This may be a 'short' time in terms of eras and epochs, but not if you're alive at the time. Paul McKaughen, president of

---

[2] Gerard Kelly, *Get A Grip On The Future Without Losing Your Hold On The Past* (Crowborough, East Sussex: Monarch, 1999).

the Evangelical Fellowship of Mission Agencies in the USA, recently said:

> I don't know of any time in my 35 years of mission experience that I have seen or felt mission executives more ready and willing to change and adapt. At the same time, I also don't know of any period in my career that there is less certainty about what changes to make. The future is uncertain. We know it will be greatly different but are not sure in which ways it will be different. We know that the patterns of the past are showing 'wear' and are in need of repair. In many ways our strategies and way of thinking do not fit our present reality very well. We know that they probably won't move us into the future God has for us. Yet the new paradigms that help us interpret and organize our strategies for the future have not become clear. We seem to be in a time of parenthesis between what God has blessed in the past and what it has yet to be made clear for the future.[3]

George Barna's description of Generation X as a 'hinge' generation means that such a transition might take up most of our working lifetime, and it will be the generations that follow us that more clearly embody the 'new world' foreseen by Drucker.

If postmodernity is a useful term by which to describe the social changes of our time, then postmodernism is a word we can use to describe the thinking and ideas that have developed around them. These ideas both create and seek to explain and understand the socio-cultural realities that we experience. In this chapter, I want to look at both the way postmodernity is shaping the experienced reality of organizational life, and also to consider how the ideas of some postmodern thinkers can be applied to bring about positive and appropriate change.

In his essay 'Impending Transformation: Mission Structures for a New Century'[4] Stanley Skreslet notes some of the cultural

---

[3] Ibid.

[4] Stanley Skreslet, 'Impending Transformation: Mission Structures for a New Century' in the *International Bulletin Of Missionary Research* 23:1 (January 1999), pp. 2–6.

changes that are impacting our world and the changing organizational realities that have developed in response to this. He roots
most changes in the phenomenon of globalization, which breaks
down boundaries of language, distance and place. As a result, he
suggests, 'these and other changes have affected the ways in
which people have taken to organize themselves socially. New
patterns of institutional life have moved to the forefront, while
other previously vital structures have faded in importance.'[5]
Among other things, he notes that the likely characteristics of a
twenty-first-century mission organization will be that they are
niche oriented and *networked*.

Niche oriented

It is a bit of a no-brainer to note that, as the world becomes more
complex, mission agencies, like businesses, are becoming
more specialized. Skreslet notes that his own denomination, the
Presbyterian Church (USA), has become much more focused in
its mission strategy, rather than trying to undertake broad
programmes. New mission organizations in the UK tend to have
a clear focus, either in terms of ministry (The Viva Network –
children at risk) or geography (Novimost – Bosnia; Partnership
For Growth – the Balkans).

Networked

The most successful new organizational structure is that of the
network. The International Campaign to Ban Landmines and
the Jubilee 2000 Debt Relief Campaign were both very loose
coalitions of organizations scattered around the world, yet which
both managed to achieve significant gains in a few years. The
anti-economic globalization movement that brought together
many thousands to protest at the World Trade Organization
meetings in Seattle in 1999 and at the G8 summit in Genoa

---

[5] Ibid. p. 2.

in 2001 were organized on a similar scale, and they didn't even bother with having a name for themselves. In my previous organization, Global Connections, for whom I worked as Associate Director for six years, we derived real organizational understanding and strength by applying the network principle to ourselves and by using the insights of management thinkers such as Charles Handy to help us understand what such a networked organization can and cannot do.

Missiologists like Andrew Walls and David Bosch have shown us how the modern Protestant missionary movement took off when it adopted an organizational form from its wider cultural context, that is, by the formation of voluntary societies. We do not need to fear using the organizational forms of our own time as valid means of structuring ourselves. A network is a very appropriate organizational form for Generation Xers, for it allows diversity to exist and flourish. It does however require approaches to leadership and management very different from the old command and control mechanisms and brings its own challenges in terms of maintaining focus and direction. No one organizational structure is perfect – each brings its own strengths and weaknesses. It is rather a matter of selecting the one that is most appropriate for the context of our work today.

Postmodern thought and organizational form

Earlier in this chapter I drew the distinction between postmodernity and postmodernism. So far we have looked briefly at how the changing socio-cultural context that we call postmodernity might influence organizational form and structure. For the rest of this chapter, I want to apply some of the insights of postmodernism – that is, the philosophical movement that has reflected upon the reality of postmodernity – to the challenge of creating mission agencies that will facilitate rather than hinder Generation Xers in their involvement in world mission.

Michel Foucault and team diversity

One of the key issues presented in this book is the issue of diversity. As the first generation primarily shaped by postmodernity rather than modernity, Generation Xers introduce challenge of diversity into organizations. They are also a diverse generation in themselves. The internationalization of the mission movement introduces a further factor of complexity, as people of different gender, generation and culture all now try to work together. So diversity is a key issue to be addressed for the successful management of mission organizations in the future.

The French postmodern philosopher and writer Michel Foucault gives us some insights that we can use to address this concern.[6] He was particularly concerned with the diversity of reality and believed that any attempt to define what is 'normal' is often a use of power that marginalizes, excludes or alienates those who don't fit the prescribed definition of 'normal'. Attempts to define Generation Xers as a 'problem' because they don't fit the 'normal' expectations of missionary life, but instead produce the conflicts described earlier in this book, are good examples of this (mis)use of power.

Foucault used the concept of *discourse* as a way of describing different world views or cultures, concepts which themselves are very familiar to those within the missionary movement. The difference between discourse and world view is that discourses 'know nothing of one another or exclude one another',[7] and so are more consciously about power. At this point some may wish to protest that the perceived problem of Generation X in relation to mission agencies is not about power – there is no attempt being made to control Generation Xers. At this point I could observe

---

[6] I am indebted to 'Dynamic Teams: Utilising Michel Foucault's Power/Resistance Matrix as a Model for Mission Teams Faced with Heterogeneity', unpublished MA dissertation by Jamie Wood, All Nations Christian College (UK), 1998, for much of the material in this section.

[7] Michel Foucault quoted in D. Macey, *The Lives Of Michel Foucault* (London: Hutchison, 1993), p. 244.

that while no intentional power play may be being made, it is certainly experienced as such by many Generation X missionaries. In addition, Foucault helps us to analyse the diffuse, unidentified, unintended or unconscious use of power, by helping us to ask 'Who says it has to be that, and not this?' He did not think of power as something used by the strong to dominate the weak, but rather saw it as simply a phenomenon of all human relationships. 'Power is not something present at specific locations within (human) networks, but is instead always at issue in ongoing attempts to (re)produce effective social alignments or to avoid or erode their effects, often by producing various counteralignments.'[8] One could quite legitimately view this book as an attempt to use the power of knowledge, experience and reason to create the social conditions in which Generation X missionaries can function effectively. This does not mean that you can use this observation to excuse your own (mis)use of power in rejecting this attempt!

Foucault's ultimate aim was to articulate and promote that which is different so as to challenge that which is considered normal. This is ultimately anti-authoritarian, and he sought to encourage the articulation of different discourses so as to reveal the arbitrary nature of every rule and norm. He called this the power/resistance matrix. Thus he encouraged the expression of different opinions, simply as an end in themselves, and not because by such airing of different views might some nearer approximation to truth or reality be discovered. One might reasonably ask what the result of such a cacophony of divergent opinions would produce – would it be confusion, chaos or anarchy? On this point Foucault was unconcerned, as he simply wanted to encourage the free expression of discourses so as to highlight the often arbitrary nature of that which rules as 'normal'.

No philosophical system can be given ultimate authority in our understanding of life. The Bible provides us with a means by

---

[8] G. Gutting, *A Cambridge Companion To Foucault* (Cambridge: Cambridge University Press, 1996), pp. 109–10.

which to evaluate all ways of viewing life and reality. Sometimes it judges those world views, challenging their assumptions and showing where they have been corrupted by endemic human fallenness. At other times, a world view or discourse can help us to see things we had not previously seen in the Bible, or understood properly. Many of us will be able to testify to the value of reading the Bible together with Christians of other cultures and the way that such exercises have helped to see anew, or maybe for the first time, new aspects of life in Christ.

In the same way, the above material on Foucault does not require us to adopt his world view wholesale or uncritically. But it can help us to understand more clearly the way that power works in definitions of what is 'normal'. It should not be hard for us to accept that sin permeates to the very heart of all human relationships. What is often difficult is seeing it in the way that *we* conduct *our* relationships (or, getting really personal, the way that I conduct mine and you conduct yours).

Jesus resisted the religious norms of his day, refusing to share in or endorse the religious traditions that had grown up over several centuries in a real attempt to be faithful to Yahweh. After all, unfaithfulness had led to the tragedy of exile, and so it was quite reasonable to try to prevent that from happening again. But such norms as had been defined led to the exclusion of many (including the Gentiles or nations) from the community of God's people. This had not necessarily been intentional, but does serve to illustrate Foucault's contention that norms, by their very nature, marginalize some and so are an exercise in power. Jesus' use of parables precluded easy interpretation and definition, so preventing us from turning them into an alternative 'norm', and his deliberate acts against the Law (such as healing on the Sabbath and associating with the outcasts and 'sinners') can be seen as a good example of Foucault's power/resistance matrix in action.

What does this mean in practice for the structures and organizational lives of mission agencies? At the very least, it means the encouragement of diversity and of the free exchange of opinions and views, not so that a reasonable compromise can be arrived at, but so that the unseen and unintended power plays at work behind all normal operating principles and procedures can be exposed and challenged. At the very least, people must be encouraged to ask, 'Who says it has to be that, and not this?' The answers given should not be an excuse or a fudge, but an honest facing of reality. You can rest assured that if you have any Generation Xers in your organization, they will not be afraid to ask such questions! The goal is not to arrive at a new, more inclusive compromise, because this will inevitably become the next set of norms that exclude and marginalize. A continual asking of questions will be necessary to prevent this. But in a world of rapid and (apparently) continual change, what other choice do we have?

The role of the leader is also affected by this thinking. We noted earlier that it is possible to see only anarchy and chaos as the outcomes of Foucault's way of thinking. In order to retain some stability or focus, it is therefore going to be necessary to have someone in the role of facilitator or coordinator. However, their role would not be to direct, but to help the rest of the team fulfil their potential and vision. This is hardly new in terms of management theory, albeit to recognize that sometimes the role of such a coordinator will be to ensure the power relationships within an organization do not become imbalanced, and to allow that their own power can be challenged.

Gilles Deleuze, chaos and leadership

Less well known than some other postmodern philosophers, Gilles Deleuze (1925–95) was Professor of Philosophy at the University of Paris VIII, Saint Denis. He sought to apply some of the ideas of chaos theory and complexity theory to the study of systems and human organization.

Chaos theory was developed to explain the function of systems that did not fit into the traditional theories of 'closed' and 'open random' systems. Closed systems provide the classical image of nature as a determinate system, a perfectly constructed watch that functions with regularity and order according to its maker's instructions. The problem with this is that everything becomes predetermined and you have to resort to Descartes' mind–body dualism to retain some concept of human freedom. The alternative, the 'open random' system, is a model of unpredictability, and offers the classic image of chaos. But neither nature nor human behaviour follows this pattern either. Everything we encounter seems to operate in some 'middle space' between these two concepts, with both order and freedom. Chaos/complexity theory developed the idea of the 'open self-organizing' system, to help understand and explain this 'middle space'.

Systems (including human organizations) exhibit characteristics of both consistency and continuity (like the 'closed' system) as well as fluctuation and change (like the 'open random' system) at the same time. This has been called the 'Noah Effect' and the 'Joseph Effect'.[9] The Noah Effect emphasizes discontinuity, where change is almost arbitrarily fast, and not necessarily smooth. Things can change massively, and almost instantaneously (the fall of the Berlin Wall, perhaps?). The Joseph Effect is about persistence – things change slowly over time – and explains longer-term growth or decline (seven years of plenty followed by seven years of drought, for example). Both these effects can work in different directions, so trends can be real, but can also vanish as quickly as they came. The end result, and the core formula of chaos theory, is 'short-term predictability, long-term unpredictability'.

In the very first verses of Genesis we are introduced to a picture of God and the world in relation to chaos (Genesis 1:2). Notwithstanding the allusions to Babylonian creation myths, and the polemic intent of Genesis 1 in showing the power of God *vis-à-vis* the pagan gods of the nations surrounding Israel, we can note that the creation narratives also show God bringing massive diversity into being, with some degree of order rather than disorder.[10] Before we conclude that God is not therefore a big fan of chaos theory, we

---

[9] James Gleick, *Chaos* (London: Vintage, 1998), pp. 92–4.

[10] 'Knowledge of these myths has laid a false trail for us, diverting our attention from the familiar fact that God's *normal* method is to work from the formless to the formed.' Derek Kidner, *Commentary On Genesis* (Leicester: IVP, 1967), p. 45.

should note the idea of the 'strange attractor', an important concept in chaos theory. This is the internal force in complex systems that constrains disorder, channelling it into patterns with some underlying theme. It brings order where none should exist, not by imposing it from outside, but by generating it from within. This in effect sums up chaos theory, for where we might suppose disorder exists, we find order, not externally imposed, but self-organized. It does not mean the celebration of disorder, but rather that recognition that order is often formed internally within complex systems, rather than being imposed from outside.

We catch intriguing glimpses of divine ambivalence towards the imposition of external order on to a situation in the original intent that Israel should not have a king to rule over them, but rather would have judges, that is, charismatic individuals who rose to prominence and leadership in times of great need, and who (usually) disappeared into obscurity again afterwards. When they did not (as for example in Gideon's case), it usually ended in tears (Judges 8:22–7). The Old Testament writers also view David's census of Israel's troops with suspicion. Whether incited by the Lord's anger (2 Samuel 24:1) or by Satan (1 Chronicles 21:1), the outcome was the same – divine punishment. In some way not clearly explained, David's attempt to create some order is not viewed positively in this case.

It is this concern about the imposition of order and structure that concerned Deleuze too. Writing in the late 1960s, he noted that Fascism came from a forced choice between disorder and state-imposed order (*après nous, la deluge*). Instead, he argued, self-organizing reality does not need external form to organize its supposed chaos. But this self-organization carries with it a 'transcendental illusion', that is, the appearance of a transcendent organizing agent coming down from on high to organize a chaotic matter, whereas it in fact comes from within. In Nazism, it looks like Hitler swooped down to save the masses from disorder – indeed, argued Deleuze, it is what Hitler wanted it to look like, and what he himself probably thought was the case.

Chaos theory suggests that changes come about because chaotic/complex systems are highly sensitive to initial conditions (hence the classic line from chaos theory: 'A butterfly flaps its wings in China and there's a tornado in America'). A small change can push a system across a 'bifurcation point' into new, radically different, behaviour. Gleick suggests this is creative, not destructive, for it allows growth to be constant and varied.[11] It also suggests interesting possibilities and approaches towards change management. For one thing, it would be nice to know what those small changes are that push systems into new behaviours. While this is something of a Holy Grail for our time, it does help us to recognize that often it is the small things that we do that bring the biggest changes, whereas some of our grand schemes leave the cosmic order pretty much undisturbed. One of the most helpful comments made to me in a previous job was that I was 'planting seeds', the fruit of which may not be immediately evident, but which would be real none the less. This can be strong encouragement when we are in difficult situations where change seems impossible, and also restrains our egos when we think that the future of the world is down to our ability to save it by lunchtime.

Viv Thomas suggests that chaos must be embraced, not feared. He quotes Mitchell Waldrop, who describes the edge of chaos as the 'one place where a complex system can be spontaneous, adaptive and alive'. Attempts to find a stable equilibrium will fail. (Gleick notes the same with regard to ecology – equilibrium, or a steady state, equals death.)[12] Great leaders, suggests Thomas, drive away from stability into chaos. Regular innovation comes through instability. Any sense of arrival will be dangerous complacency.[13]

To conclude, rather than simply seeking the one 'unifying paradigm' that will help us to organize the future, critically drawing on postmodern thought allows us to embrace multiple ideas about the future. We need to work towards F. Scott Fitzgerald's idea of a first class mind: 'the ability to hold two

---

[11] Gleick, *Chaos*, p. 311.
[12] Ibid. p. 315.
[13] Viv Thomas, *Future Leader* (Carlisle: Paternoster, 1999), pp. 77–9.

opposing ideas in the head at the same time, and still retain the ability to function'.[14] Diversity is not a problem to be solved, but a reality to be embraced.

[14] Quoted in Charles Handy, *The Empty Raincoat* (London: Hutchinson 1994), p. 18.

Part 3

Man on the moon
(How do we achieve the impossible?)

7

We are family

Creating good intergenerational relationships in organizations

Sarah Hay

There's a feeling within Christian organizations, such as mission agencies, that since we are all Christians working together we should all therefore relate as one big, happy family. As previous chapters have outlined, however, such organizations have their fair share of interpersonal problems and are very often not the big, happy family. This is hardly surprising when we look at the average family, which also suffers through lack of time, stress, and (dare I say it) intergenerational issues, amongst other things. A truly functional family, where every member is valued, despite their age and outlook, can be a good model for organizations to aim at, however.

Of course, there are other issues that prevent a mission organization from being effective. Some of these issues are cultural, having a direct effect on interpersonal relationships. Others are, for example, denomination, country of birth and gender. There is much written on the effects of different cultures working together within a team. But the importance of generational issues must not be underestimated in the organization's attempt to improve. Here we will focus on generational factors and how we can attempt to facilitate different generations to work together. Firstly, however, a couple of questions.

Why not go it alone?

Rather than working together, why don't we just go it alone, separate the generations, and form agencies for Xers? We have 'Youth With A Mission' (complete with an array of Boomers!) so why not form 'Xers Xtreme' (their slogan could be 'Reaching the lands the oldies dare not go – on skateboards!'), 'Nexters New Mission', and other organizations for specific generations? Everyone could then be of the same mind and reach out to people of like culture. Makes sense, doesn't it. Or does it? I believe that an organization with a variety of generations working together can be far more effective than one made up of one type of person only. The youngsters are not tainted with traditions. They carry less baggage simply because they have had less time to gather it. They challenge the norm in an organization often because they have not been there long enough to realize that it is the norm. The 'Veterans' within the team can bring stability and helpful insight through their experience and help to challenge and channel the younger people's motivation and new ideas. If they see and accept the strengths and weaknesses of one another they can work together; the young challenging the norm with their new ideas, insights and suggestions; the Veterans challenging the ideas of the young with their past experiences. If they can recognize their complementary roles they can change the traditional for something that is honed and tested by both groups. The mission world therefore needs its Veterans and seniors to share their experience with the younger generations. It needs the younger generations to bring creativity, enthusiasm and ideas. But it needs everyone to have grace and humility to recognize their own limitations and the gifts of others.

If we take the Bible as a guide, we also see examples here of communities working and living together, where there would have been people of different generations included. We talk about '*koinonia*' – from the Greek root 'to share' or 'have in common'. We share the same Spirit and are urged to make 'every effort to maintain the unity of the Spirit in the bond of peace' (Ephesians 4:3). There should therefore be no place for division due to generation. The church is described as a family, again showing that different generations are present. In 1 Thessalonians 4: 9–10, Paul urges the brothers to love each other more and more. This is surely a good model for us to follow: to work and live together, and not create more division. There has been much discussion in the Christian world about the church being 'community' and I believe that there is value in the mission agencies attempting to become more community-like also. M. Scott Peck, in his book *The Different Drum*, describes a community as 'a group of individuals who have learned how to communicate honestly with each other, whose relationships go deeper than their mask of composure, and who have developed some significant commitment to "rejoice together, mourn together," and to "delight in each other, make others' conditions our own." '[1] As we seek to further God's Kingdom, it would seem that this is a good model to aim for. It encourages us to work together, not alone, and to build each other up so that we can be strong and more able to do what God has asked of us. As an individual, I may be able to reach out to a few, but if I team up effectively with a few others, I will be able to reach much further. So let's not go it alone.

All things weird and wonderful

OK, so we'll try to work together. But some people are too difficult / different / independent / annoying / irritating / just plain weird* (*delete as appropriate)! Do they have to be included? Can't we just stick to people like us within our organization? We've all met Christians who we don't get on with (admit it!) or who we'd rather not be seen with. When my husband and I went to Nepal, I was determined that we would not look like a 'traditional missionary couple' – no long plait, straw hat and twinset for me, and Rob was forbidden from growing a beard! Yet God is in the business of calling all kinds of people to follow

---

[1] M. Scott Peck, *The Different Drum* (London: Arrow, 1997), p. 59.

him and to work for him. Jesus, during his time on earth, specialized in meeting with the outcasts of community – the lepers, the adulterous women, the children, the poor and the disabled. We must therefore be careful not to limit God's work by screening out of our mission organizations people who we think won't fit in, just because they are not like us. Of course we need to have good recruitment and selection processes so that only those who can cope with the stresses of missionary life are sent to the field, but we should be wary of recruiting the same type of people who have always been selected. The danger of the 'round hole and square peg' scenario is that perhaps it is the hole that is the wrong shape, not the peg (that is, we may be looking for the wrong type of person, and so miss the most suitable applicant).

Can we fix it? Yes we can!

In the words of the beloved British children's TV character, Bob the Builder, 'Can we fix it?' Yes we can! There is clearly a problem when different generations try to work together, but there are ways to fix the problem. Every organization is different and so solutions may vary, but I will attempt below to outline some ways in which we can fix the problems caused by intergenerational differences. I am by no means an expert and should make it clear that I am a thirty-one-year-old (how old?) Generation Xer who sometimes thinks she is more of a Boomer! But I have worked as a personnel professional in organizations made up of people across the spectrum of generations and hope that I have some experience that may be useful to draw upon. (Some of these pointers could also be utilized in interpersonal problems caused by factors other than generation.)

Relationships

The key to the problem is, perhaps rather obviously, relationships. This may not be rocket science or a revelation of a deep mystery, but it is vital that we invest time and energy into the relationships that we have with each other. We will get along better and be able to work better with others if we know them, understand where they are coming from and can respect them for their differences.

When a new missionary goes out to the field, we emphasize to them the importance of 'acculturation', that is, the importance of acquiring cultural sensitivity and language. It would have been no use if I had gone straight out to Nepal without the knowledge that my culture was different from that of the host culture. If I had not spent time going through a strong period of orientation, learning about these cultural differences, I would have upset many relationships with Nepalese friends by eating with my left hand, pointing at things with my feet, and stepping over people on my way to the space on the floor that was to be my 'pew' in church. (I still made cultural blunders, but there's no space for that now!) We also spend a lot of time trying to learn the new language of the country that we are in. My biggest frustration in Nepal was how poor my language was and how much this affected me in being able to communicate and build good relationships with local people. If you spend a lot of time communicating (some may say I talk a lot!) then this is very debilitating.

Yet, despite these efforts at acculturation, we fail to encourage this *within* our organizations. If we spend time trying to understand the culture of other generations, if we learn how they might tackle different issues, if we try to respect their differing viewpoints, then we just might be able to improve our relationships with them. We should encourage open and supportive relationships and make it easier for these differing groups to talk. Look at your orientation programme (both for overseas and home staff). Encourage dialogue between generations. New recruits often feel totally 'at sea' in a new environment where they are the new kids on the block. It is believed that they are the ones who need to be taught everything and listen to 'how we do things around here'. The result is that they often end up feeling even more alone and isolated and feel disempowered to do anything or try anything new once they have finished the orientation programme. So try not to smother new staff with 'we always do things like this', but rather ask them for their thoughts and their reactions. You could use scenarios and ask them to discuss how they may have dealt with the situation, rather then just telling them what you may have done. Also, place importance on the skills and experience that they are bringing. After all, they were recruited because they had something to offer. (If they didn't, why did you take them on?)

While we're on the subject of orientation for new recruits, you may also want to look at reorientation for your current staff. Some people may have been in your organization for a long time and know little about generational issues. It would be wise to spend time with them, discussing such differences, and encouraging them to be open and willing to accept the differences that new recruits and people from different generations may bring. Again, the model to look at would be that of Jesus. He had special relationships with a variety of people and spent much time with them. Our relationship with him should also be based on dialogue, openness and honesty, and this is something that should be encouraged between generations.

Communication

Communication must be mentioned because it is key to relationships, but it is something that many organizations (and individuals) are bad at. In order to build good relationships, we must encourage good communication. Zemke, Raines and Filipczak talk about 'aggressive communication'.[2] This means that you should anticipate and then 'surface' any generational and potential conflicts that there may be. By 'surfacing' or identifying these conflict areas, you are taking a huge step towards resolving them. It is like the alcoholic who finally sees that he or she has a problem. It's only then that they can start to work on it. By identifying the problems and encouraging people to discuss them

---

[2] Zemke, Raines and Filipczak, *Generations At Work*, p. 153.

you can channel the energy that would have gone into 'behind-the-back' complaining, whinging and even open hostility into communication with each other and projects that could benefit from the different viewpoints. Some discussions may well need facilitation to enable each person to air their views. It will also be important to validate the different viewpoints, not enabling one to be seen as more 'right' or superior to another.

For different generations to work together there needs to be acceptance that we all have different views that can be complementary and not conflicting. Recently, a group of missionaries were asked whether they would like a small increase in their allowance. The older generations did not want an increase, saying that they had too much money already, whilst the younger generations (and especially those with small children) welcomed the idea. The different viewpoints were interesting. The older people had learnt to live with a simple lifestyle and did not feel the need to take a holiday or trip home, whilst the younger people would have valued the chance to go on holiday to a neighbouring country, to take a trip home or to be able to take their children regularly to a local swimming pool. The outlooks were very different according to generation, so what to do? The older members, whilst not needing the extra money they already had for day-to-day living, were putting it towards a pension, into a savings account, giving it away or using it for more regular trips home as they started to consider retirement and reintegration. Thus, if the allowance was increased, they could still use the money, though in a different way to the young families. So through dialogue and understanding, all generations were catered for, though they saw the situation in different ways.

I believe that you can never overcommunicate. So often in the jobs that I have had in the past I have heard the moan 'My manager has just changed this and never asked my opinion.' Integrated staff meetings are useful, as are staff newsletters and so on. In INF (International Nepal Fellowship) we regularly had a newsletter from the International Council informing us of any major decisions that had been taken or major initiatives that they were beginning to look into. This type of communication was greatly appreciated. The smaller, ad hoc, group discussions and discussions in the kitchen or over the water cooler or even the coffee machine are also important though, and so our organizational culture should not frown on general chat (within reason, of course). These chats enable people to get to know each other and will hopefully help to form better relationships. As well as disseminating information, however, communication should include as much listening as talking. People need to feel that they have been listened to and that, where possible, their thoughts and ideas have been taken on board. This is especially so for the Generation Xer.

Co-existence

As I have already hinted, it is vital that our mission agencies encourage an environment where all generations can live and work together, co-existing. Assisting each group to understand and value the others should discourage the idea of 'them and us'. This is easy to say and far less easy to achieve, but facilitating dialogue is important. Team days, away days and such like can be useful. My husband led an away day for a large team of people from differing generations whilst we were in Nepal, and found that it was very useful, but that he had to allow time for the airing of hugely differing views. It was important for him, as the facilitator, to remain objective and show no bias towards the views that he personally held. The result, however, was a diverse team who worked fairly well together, given the very different personalities and ages present.

The following chart, compiled from material in *Generations At Work* by Zemke, Raines and Filipczak (mentioned earlier) outlines the strengths and weaknesses of each generation, and may serve as a useful guide.

Generation	Approximate Birth Dates	Generational Personality	Heroes	Asset	Liabilities
VETERANS	1920–45	They like consistency and uniformity They like things on a grand scale They are conformers They believe in logic, not magic They are disciplined They are past-oriented and history-absorbed They have always believed in law and order Their spending style is conservative	Superman Franklin D. Roosevelt Winston Churchill Montgomery Patton Eisenhower	Stable Detail-oriented Thorough Loyal Hard-working	Inept with ambiguity and change Reluctant to buck the system Uncomfortable with conflict Reticent when they disagree
BOOMERS	1945–65	They believe in growth and expansion They think of themselves as stars of the show They tend to be optimistic They have learnt about teamwork They have pursued their own personal gratification, uncompromisingly, and often at a high price to themselves and others They have searched their souls – repeatedly, obsessively and recreationally They have always been cool – ask one!	Gandhi Martin Luther King John F. Kennedy	Service-oriented Driven Willing to 'go the extra mile' Good at relationships Want to please Good team players	Not naturally 'budget minded' Uncomfortable with conflict Reluctant to go against peers May put process ahead of result Overly sensitive to feedback Judgemental of those who see things differently Self-centred
GENERATION X	1965–80	They are self-reliant They are seeking a sense of family They want balance They have a nontraditional orientation about time and space They like informality Their approach to authority is casual They are sceptical They are attracted to the edge They are technologically savvy	None	Adaptable Technoliterate Independent Unintimidated by authority Creative	Impatient Poor people skills Inexperienced Cynical

For individuals, all need to try and remain open and willing to accept that there will be differences. For the managers, they need to be willing to act as facilitators and have a leadership style that is appropriate.

Leadership style

For any manager within the mission world, be they managing one or two people or a much larger team, care must be taken over the style of leadership that they employ. Younger generations do not appreciate a directive style and want a manager who is approachable, willing to listen and willing to involve others in their decision making. Because leaders need experience, it is often the case that leaders are of a different, older, generation than some of the people that they are managing. Thus some organizations will need to help to develop their leaders, providing them with good training and encouragement to think through issues differently. This is not always easy. I led an away day for the International Council of INF entitled 'People-Centred Leadership'. The aim was to highlight the role that the personnel department could hold and the need for the leadership style of INF to be more people focused (people being the members and staff). I felt that the day went well. One of the sessions, however, was based on some of the problems that an average INF member may face, for example, housing issues, loneliness, homesickness, illness, education of children issues, and so on, all of which, if not tackled, could result in a member leaving Nepal prematurely. I sensed that there were some present who were shocked at some of the problems that I had listed, not realizing that, for some, these were big issues. Among the older members of the group, I felt that there was a tendency for them to believe that these issues should not have been a problem, and that the younger, newer members just hadn't learnt how to live sacrificially and were making mountains out of molehills. Yet for some, these issues were truly huge. The key is to get people to understand the viewpoint of others, learn to accept that view and help them to deal with it, rather than just treating it as a non-problem.

Leadership style will not be changed overnight but more openness and dialogue (as mentioned above) is vital. It is also important that organizations seek to employ some younger leaders from the generations that they are seeking to attract.

In *Generations at Work*, Zemke, Raines and Filipczak also talk about 'difference deployment'. This is where leaders make tactical use of employees with different backgrounds, skills and so on. Too often, organizations employ people who are all the same (round pegs for their round holes). This is the safe option but may result in a staff group who are not thinking ahead, looking to the future and challenging the working method. A team needs to have different skills and expertise so that it can remain on the cutting edge. Perhaps we need to employ some square pegs who can change the round hole!

Years ago, we were involved in running a church youth group. There had been a number of problems and the leaders met up to discuss the way forward. We encouraged everyone to think about what they were good at and where they thought their skills lay. As we shared, we realized that we had all been trying to be good at everything. We had been trying to fill what we thought the mould for 'youth leader' should be, rather than deploying our differences and skills into the right areas. We reassigned our tasks so that only Nick, the loud, bubbly, joker, was the one who did the welcome and large group sessions, whilst Rob planned the main social activities, Tim prepared the Bible study materials, Lynne and I chatted and befriended the girls (no guessing what our skills were!) and so on. After that, leading the youth group took on a new joy, as we were all freed into only doing what we were good at, and yet all were complementing the whole. Organizations and teams can do the same if we are all open with each other and if the leaders are willing to take a risk or two.

Leadership styles that attract Xers will not be fixed but able to give direction and then leave the actual workings out to the individuals. The leader will need to learn to give feedback, reward and recognition where appropriate and place more emphasis on concern for the team members, rather than just on the team output. Some organizations go so far as to treat their employees as customers, learning about them, what their needs are, how they prefer to work and so on, so that they can build more friendly working practices. There is a growing trend for family-friendly policies too.

For those who are not leaders, it would be helpful to accept that the role of a leader is not easy and that you need to co-operate and make suggestions in helpful ways (and learn from the experience, because you may be tomorrow's leader!).

Mentoring

Mentoring is a good way of encouraging generations to work together. The idea is rather like that of an apprenticeship system. Webster's dictionary describes a mentor as 'a trusted counselor or guide'. A mentor can be a role model, showing someone the ropes, listening to current problems, and giving both advice and constructive criticism, using their resources developed through experience. In the mission context, the mentor may be able to guide through not only work issues but also cultural and even spiritual issues. The mentor needs to facilitate rather than simply instruct. Although not widely used in the mission sector at present, those people who have used the system are delighted with its results. A friend who works in a large mission organization has had a mentor now for several years. She has found the relationship invaluable, giving her the confidence to step out of her comfort zone and achieve amazing things, so much so that she is now a leader and mentor herself. Her own mentoring does not stop there, however. She continues to be mentored and her relationship with that older person is still strong.

The beauty of mentoring is that it enables us Xers to learn from our elders in helpful, constructive ways, and will hopefully build into us a respect for them, rather than frustration. It should create stronger relationships and a mutual respect between the generations.

Reconciliation

Much of what I have said so far has assumed that people are willing to work at improving relationships. But in many organizations there will be people who are hurting because of poor relationships. Others may be angry ('He's always treating me as if I'm a child'), frustrated ('Why won't she give me a chance'), bitter (I've had it with them), and so on. For the above ideas to work, these broken or hurting relationships need to be dealt with first. There needs to be reconciliation and forgiveness.

Obviously, this is easy to say on paper but much harder to achieve in practice. People may need to be made aware of the hurts (both within themselves and within others). Various questions need to be asked: who do I need to forgive for hurting me (possibly even unknowingly); who do I need to ask forgiveness of; which people may I have hurt? The process of forgiving and being reconciled may take time, requiring a constant return to forgiveness (even though God's forgiveness is complete, it is also ongoing). It may also need help from someone outside of the situation, both to help identify the hurts and then bring people together to discuss the issues, understand each other, forgive and then move on to a new relationship with each other. This person's role may just be to listen, but that is important. If the hurts are deep, ongoing pastoral care may also be required. Our God is a truly forgiving Father and wants us to be in good relations with each other. He is full of grace – something that we need to learn to build into our own relationships with each other.

The reconciliation business is tough. It may be that in helping people to face up to the issues there will be some casualties. I believe that mission organizations still have responsibility for these people, even if they do leave, and every attempt should be made to help them in terms of debriefing, linking up with good pastoral support, and so on. Too often when people leave, the mission organization breathes a sigh of relief. There may of course, as I have experienced, be situations where people have left an organization filled with hurt and have refused offers of assistance, debriefing and counselling. There is nothing more that can be done then, but at least the organization has fulfilled its responsibility as best it can.

Common vision

During my time in INF I became aware that some of the generational issues related to vision and 'calling'. This was not solely generational, but largely so. There were those who felt called to mission somewhere in the world, others called specifically to Nepal, and others called to a particular town or people group. Then there were those who saw their profession as a means solely for entering the country and enabling them to work alongside churches (mainly the Veterans) and others who saw their profession and work as their main focus, church involvement being a minor issue in which they participated if they had the time (mainly the Xers). This did cause some friction. We personally spent a lot of time in our INF roles and our involvement in church was mainly just going along each week. But when some expatriates there asked us what we were doing in church, and we told them, there was a disapproving look and an unspoken pressure to become more involved.

This difference in vision and calling can cause friction and it may be helpful for the organization to look into this and perhaps undertake some teaching, Bible studies and so on in this area, to help people become aware of the differences and respect others. Whilst the immediate vision may be different, each person has been asked by God to work for him.

DIY relationships

I hope that the above points will be helpful to those in managerial and leadership positions in our mission agencies. There will, of course, be other methods that can be used and different organizations will have different problems and therefore different solutions.

I am aware that I have been speaking mainly to leaders and from a personnel professional viewpoint. I have not really tackled how you, as an individual, may improve your own relationships with people from differing generations. But the above principles can be applied to you, as well as to the organization you are in. You need to be open, honest and respectful in your relationships, maintaining good communication and learning to work with others. If you're not a leader, you need to think about how it may be for the people managing you, and try to remain open. Also, you must be aware of any forgiveness issues and seek reconciliation where necessary.

As I have said before, these pointers should not be revolutionary. Much is simple common sense. But often when we are stuck in a rut of poor relationships it can be hard to see the way ahead. If you do nothing else, look to Jesus. As he is the Way, I pray that he may equip you with all you need to continue on your journey. Happy travelling.

8

Don't throw the baby out with the bath water

Changing an organization's culture

Rob Hay

Don't skip this chapter.

You've read this far, you've listened to the clashes Xers have experienced with mission agencies, you've read about the difficulties of intergenerational relationships and you have heard first-hand accounts of people's struggles and challenges. You have also hopefully caught something of the people's passion for Jesus Christ and his mission and the amazing opportunity that postmodernity presents. It's tempting to throw the baby out with the bath water, to ditch the existing, go with the new and start over. Whether you're an Xer who's so frustrated with the status quo that you want to jack it all in and start again, a Boomer who's fed up with Xers and wants to let them get out of the way, or a Veteran who is so weary at the thought of another generation that it's tempting just to sit back and wait for retirement – don't skip this chapter! There is too much to lose.

There is too much to be lost to the mission of Jesus by ditching all our existing organizations and starting over. At Holy Island we divided into two groups: 'Starting from scratch' and 'Renewing the existing organization'. About 70 per cent wanted to focus on renewing the existing. For myself, perhaps inevitably with my consultancy background, I wanted to renew, although I confess I wanted at least a few looking at starting over just in case we couldn't make the renewal work. Besides a professional stance that believes almost any organization can be changed, my other motivation for renewing is a less logical one. Diverse organizations are always more demanding to lead (my own project in Nepal covered thirteen professional areas, seven locations and fifteen nationalities!) and are almost certainly not the most efficient, but they are potentially the most effective and they are more godly. No, not more holy. More God-like – more like God. The modern world and particularly the advertising world may tell us that niching, tribalism, the grouping together of like peoples is the preferred norm but God declares that diversity is his norm, indeed, his gift.

We are convinced that renewing is making the best use of what God has given us in an organization and that we lose so much by starting over that this should not be the first choice. There are many good books on change management, and we don't have space here to cover that process anyway. I hope to describe some of my experiences in health sector management in the UK and in Nepal to highlight a few areas that are often neglected or underestimated in the process.

Recognize people

There are very few people who do not need to feel that their contribution is valued. Psychology tells us that this is essential to a healthy life. However, in Christian circles, particularly in mission, we focus on sacrifice and an unspoken view that as long as God values what we do, that is all that matters. There is a place for sacrificial giving of oneself in the Christian faith but there is no place for not valuing people – indeed Scripture challenges us to see others as God sees them.

In one role I coined the phrase 'Big Personalities'. These were a small number of incredibly skilled and clever people with heaps of energy, vision and often charisma, but who were usually a nightmare to manage. Programmes they ran were usually known as *their* programmes. The structures and systems on which the programme worked was usually informal and bypassed the formal structures. Much of the funding came because of the person leading it. You probably know a few such people yourself. They often come across as determined to the point of being aggressive and distanced to the point of separation. However, if you listened to them, they had often not felt fully used or valued in the organization, and had seized an opportunity to do something they were good at and had run it separately, across the formal structures and in breach of formal procedures, only because they had to. They knew what they were doing was valuable but they were doing it in spite of the organization rather than through and with the support of the organization. These people were often leaders in their field nationally, if not internationally, but were often working on something that, whilst it may have been groundbreaking, was at the fringe of what the organization was trying to do.

On the other end of the scale there was the white elephant programme that was felt to be core to the organization and reflected its aims and ethos perfectly. But the person who led it had left and no one else could quite seem to catch the vision and lead the programme in quite the same way.

People are our greatest resource, our most valuable asset. That is not just a phrase – it is the truth. But too often we stop there and need to remind ourselves that they are an asset to the organization, or should be. To be effective we need to recognize people, their hopes, dreams, calling and aspirations and empower and facilitate them to fulfil those hopes in such a way as to meet the aims and goals of the organization.

When you attempt to bring change, you must remember that any work you change will be the fruit of someone's hopes, dreams, sacrifices and efforts. It will provoke strong feelings and resistance to change – if it doesn't, it is probably a white elephant that should have been buried sometime back anyway. When you are considering how your change might affect the people concerned, imagine spending one year of your life bringing these changes and then have someone come and change it all back. Some of the work you will try and change may have had most of a lifetime of effort invested in it, so treat it with care.

I fear there are other occasions, but I am aware of one time when I forgot that rule. I was frustrated with one person's intransigence to change and went to bypass them as I sought to change 'their' project. It needed changing. They needed to change. My aim was right. However, I will always remember that person's face, indeed their whole body language. I had crushed them. Though I was trying to maintain and develop *the work*, I had communicated to them that *their work* was of no value. My motive may have been right, but I was wrong, and I was horrified at what I had done to that person. I owned up, backed down, said sorry and let things continue unchanged. Slowly, later on, change came, is still happening and will take a long time, but the work is not at odds with the organization, just a little different in the way it works.

However, sometimes the work is so far out of step with the aims of the organization that it should not continue where it is. Any such change is going to be radical. In INF there was one programme that was a specialized engineering area on the fringe of INF's focus, but it was none the less doing vital work for the country of Nepal. In the end, INF helped the leader set up as a private business. It was done carefully and paced at a manageable speed with ongoing advice, but it maintained the important work. Removing the project from INF yet allowing it to focus on its core aim communicated to the person leading the programme: 'This is not INF's core work but it is important work. Your work is vital. So much so that we will spend time, energy and effort helping you to do it more effectively.'

Co-ordinated and clear leadership

Change is possibly one of the hardest tasks of leadership. Doug Balfour of Tearfund shared his feelings.

The cliché is that leadership is lonely, and that's true, but my emotions changed through the process.

The first thing you feel is incredibly insecure because you are believing all the preliminary data about the problem and the size of it, and yet other people are saying you are using a massive hammer to crack a nut and that there is no problem at all. Yet there is a consciousness that God is with you and leading you to the only possible starting place.

There is a massive confidence struggle inside you. Outwardly you are having to be enormously confident, consistently saying the same thing, and inwardly you are saying 'Have I really got this right, am I going to waste all these people's time, is it going to be a terrible failure?' But my own calling to Tearfund became the cornerstone of my confidence; a foundation for the confidence that I was leading people into what might seem like a wilderness.

The feeling of loneliness in leadership is inevitable and with change, just like any other management task, having a mentor/confidante outside of the organization can be immensely helpful. If you are using a consultant/advisor to help you change the organization, use them as support. You need to because as the leader you must be careful to champion the change and champions are focused, determined and positive.

Co-ordinated change is important as well. There is nothing like contradictory messages and actions to undermine fledgling confidence in a change process.

Milestones: recognize progress

Often with change programmes, people decide what they want to achieve, map it out and off they go. The fact that it will take them a year to achieve what they want does not stop them launching with a big fanfare and planning a big party when they reach their destination. However, a year is a long time, change is an unsettling process and the road to change can seem lonely and without any markers and familiar sights on the way. People need markers. They need to be able to see progress. I have seen so many attempts to bring change that were planned well, had the right aims and would probably have worked, fall and fail because people weren't sure that they were still making progress on the right road. An individual with a vision is not always enough – they may not always be around. In Nepal, a good attempt at change failed when a key person was forced to leave the field unexpectedly. The work continued for a bit but no one was too sure of how well things were progressing: there were no waymarks, only a start and end point.

This point is not complicated but essential. Do you remember as a child going to the seaside and asking, 'Are we nearly there yet?' The first question usually came three miles from home and was repeated every fifteen minutes. My parents learnt that if they said that the Severn Bridge was half way and at Swansea we had one hour left, I did not ask nearly so often. I could look out for those landmarks, be encouraged we were progressing, and not be nearly as irritating. In Nepal, an enterprising businessman had gone a stage further. Exactly halfway between our home in Pokhara and Kathmandu, he built the closest thing to a motorway service area. For ten kilometres either side, he had signs saying '10 km to Riverside Springs', '9 km to …', '8 km …' and so on. In the middle of the dry season, on a hot motorbike with an inch of dust coating my visor, I would look for that first sign, lick my lips and then count down the kilometres until I could drink that cold Coke sitting under a fan in a comfy chair. When I left to carry on to Kathmandu, I knew that I was over halfway and on the final stage.

That's all milestones are. When you plan a change, break the journey down, put up some easy-to-see signposts that mark progress and at a couple of them put a cold Coke and a comfy chair as a reward for progress and as a refreshment for the onward journey.

Resistance is ~~futile~~ natural

An area that causes more grief to managers involved in change than any other is when they hit resistance and, in particular, individual resistors. The automatic reaction to people opposed to the changes you are attempting to implement is to see them as the opposition, as enemies to be overcome and as the biggest threat to your change endeavour. Resistance is not the biggest threat to your change efforts and resistors are not your enemies. The biggest threat to your change efforts would be ignoring what your resistors are saying and failing to understand the reasons for their resistance.

I remember a small situation many years ago in one of my early management roles that illustrates how ignoring your resistors can dramatically affect the outcome of a change effort. I took over the management of several departments in a large general hospital. My predecessor had attempted a much-needed shake up of one department: clinical coding. He had attempted to streamline the process of computer coding the operations done in the hospital. The results were evident when I took over. Throughput was down by 25 per cent, and yet he had eliminated lots of unnecessary work and effort. When I talked to the team of five girls who did the coding they felt that they had not been listened to and therefore had resisted the change despite a tacit acceptance that some changes were necessary. The key area he might have picked up if he had listened to the girls was the boredom factor. Doing data entry is boring enough, but the girls all had to be qualified to a high level in biology and anatomy, therefore were not typical data entry clerks – and they got BORED! When they got bored they slowed down, took breaks and had more sick leave. One of the things they used to do before the changes was play Trivial Pursuit – yes, the board game. They would play it all day, every day, as they worked. They said this relieved the boredom. They said they knew they worked better when they had something to think about. I reversed the decision, they started to play Trivial Pursuit again, and the throughput went up to 25 per cent above its original level. Most of his changes had been right, most had contributed to improving throughput, but in not listening to the people resisting change he steamrollered them, they rebelled and his changes seemed to have failed.

A few pointers on resistance:

- Accept the view of your resistors. Whether it is reality or just their perception, it is their starting place, and needs to be yours too.
- Acknowledge that you do not have a monopoly on reality. Your staff will know their jobs better than you do, so listen.
- Listen carefully, ask lots of questions and don't answer your own questions (see 'Communication' below).
- Give resistors your total attention. You have to earn the right to be heard by your resistors – do that by listening to them and making them feel that you have heard them.
- Find some common ground. Shared ground stops the 'them and us' mentality.
- In tackling issues that resistors have, make sure that you are focusing on the issue and not the person. Depersonalizing resistance makes it much less threatening.
- Remember that you don't solve resistance but only postpone it if you promise things you can't deliver.

Communicate, communicate, communicate

You will probably have picked up by now that communication runs through every area that we have talked about, but it is worth reminding ourselves of some principles that are particularly relevant to change efforts.

Firstly and most importantly, assume you are never communicating sufficiently. Communication (assuming it is good communication) is almost impossible to overdo in a time of change. Focus groups, feedback systems and one-to-one conversations are all forms of communication.

Two ears and one mouth

The old adage that with two ears and one mouth we should listen twice as much as we speak is especially true in leading change. Learning to ask people questions and then listen instead of answering them ourselves is difficult but important. It is especially difficult if we are greeted with silence. We need to sit out the silence and wait for people to speak. Leaders usually fill silence with their own words!

Communicate personally

In a time of major change you need to make the change efforts your main focus. You need to be seen to be leading the change. Like a general leading troops, you being at the front of the change inspires people with confidence because you are demonstrating your own wholehearted commitment to it. It also means that you need to be communicating with people at all levels in a meaningful way. If there are sceptical managers you limit their ability to influence their teams by making yourself accessible to all of their team.

Communicate truthfully

Given the limits I mentioned earlier about clear and co-ordinated leadership and having to display more confidence in the planned changes than you sometimes feel, in all other respects you need to go out of your way to ensure transparency. Making meeting notes available, opening up meetings to observers and offering question and answer sessions all help because in a time of change any whiff of ambiguity or cover-up fuels resistance, suspicion and fear.

I saw a great example of this is another mission organization in Nepal. A new leader was making radical changes, difficult decisions and wide-ranging reviews. He was doing it in the same organization where these things had been tried and failed just a short time before. I asked some of the staff why it was working this time when it hadn't before. 'We know why the changes are happening and can comment on them,' said one person, and everyone else reflected those sentiments. The leader was devoted to the change, was devoting serious time and energy to the change, and was present. This organization worked in many locations but wherever I went the answer was the same. He comes to see us. Tells us to come and talk, ask questions and voice concerns. We know we can phone him anytime. He doesn't always agree with us but he does listen and at the end of the day the difficult decisions are his and he takes the responsibility.

Finally and most importantly: communicate, communicate and communicate.

Building consensus – don't fight alone

If you define consensus as unity and seek it as a prerequisite for change, you will never start on your change journey. Likewise, consensus management is not the leadership style for a change agent, but neither is the isolationist revolutionary who waits until he or she is in position within the organization and then detonates his or her change bomb, with the expectation of some blood and casualties, but with him or her as the standard bearer of a new ethos emerging from the smoke as the hero. He or she more likely to be seen as a terrorist and expelled from the midst.

When I talk about building consensus I am saying that a change agent can rarely achieve the change alone and needs allies and supporters. The more established the system or value you try to change the more support you will need. A good example of the importance of this is an organization's logo. Logos are like names, an identity that people in and around the organization often see as synonymous with the organization itself and its values and work. Sometimes it is even more. The logo can be a graphic that, whilst it includes the initials or even the name of the organization, is recognized by and communicated to people who do not speak English. In one instance, a logo communicated to probably around twenty different people groups and local languages that a vehicle belonged to a certain organization. However, the same logo looked dated in international literature and on the organization's web site, so the decision was taken to design a new logo. The process was:

MANAGEMENT TEAM DECISION	→	DESIGN DEPARTMENT	→	PRESENTATION OF POSSIBLE DESIGNS

The outcome was rejection of the suggested new designs by the staff. I am a great believer in letting the skilled people do the job that they are skilled for and the idea of everyone getting out their pen and paper in my book is silly and an insult to the designers. However, the opportunity for your staff to contribute ideas, feelings, values and so on to the process at the start and then allow the designers to create a graphic that encompasses those feelings not only feeds the designers' ideas, but it involves the people in the process and prepares them to view and buy into a design when it is presented. In all aspects of change, think carefully how you can involve the stakeholders sufficiently to get their buy-in without compromising the roles of skilled professionals who can make it happen. The balance is difficult but essential to find.

Consensus is all about getting sufficient people 'on board' with an idea to make it work. It can significantly lengthen a change process but it will improve its chances of success. Richard Tiplady estimated that the change from Evangelical Missionary Alliance to Global Connections was a three-and-a-half-year process, and that during first eighteen months the only thing he did was prepare the ground and build consensus for the change ahead. This book and the event behind it are testimony that this was time well spent.

Consensus building is not a sales job. It is demonstrating to people the relevance of change to them and the organization, and the relevance of them to the change.

Conclusions

Don't flog a dead horse

I started by saying don't skip this chapter. I want to finish by saying you cannot change every situation you find yourself in ... even if you do everything right. As I said, I am passionate about renewing organizations, and I used to think optimistically that none were beyond reach and that giving up on a change was wrong. Experience has taught me that some situations can't be changed and the Bible teaches me that giving up on some is not wrong. Even with the full support of your key people, there simply may not be the resources in an organization to make the change. Jesus told the disciples to go into a village and speak and await a response and if there was no response to brush the dust from their feet and move on.

Companions for the journey

If you are trying to bring change but are a lone voice in your organization, you need to do a reality check. Are you right in what you are saying and trying to do? This is difficult when you are alone in an organization, but one way is to find a mentor or peer outside of the situation who has done or is doing change in their organization. This helps you to see if you are on the right track, if you should keep going, and also gives you some support and encouragement if you are and do.

One purpose of this book is to widen the network of people involved in these issues. There are forums on the associated web site, <www.postmission.com>, for this purpose. Please join them and find some fellow travellers to keep you company on your journey of change.

9

Where do we go from here?

A word from an older 'brother and sister'

Bill and Yvonne Taylor

Yvonne and I were privileged to be part of the Holy Island Roundtable in March 2001. The deep engagement of heart, mind, spirit and body with a small group of profoundly committed and gifted women and men of a younger generation was special. The days were rich and long, starting with worship that focused on some aspect of Celtic spirituality and mission. From there it was telling stories, challenging each other, listening, praying, laughing and learning how to communicate in the diverse faces of the English language with citizens of England, Ireland, Scotland, New Zealand, Sweden, Canada and the USA. Meals together, evening discussions that moved from the official venue site to the pubs, and field trips to rich Celtic sites all contributed to a profound sense of oneness out of our valued diversity. We were asked to be present as elders, to listen, to pray, to worship, to respond when asked, and then to speak with freedom from our hearts.

That's what we want to do in this last chapter – speak from our heart/mind to the hearts/minds of our readers from both the younger and older generations. We belong to the 'older' ones, with three Generation X children born and raised in Latin America, who have been influenced in diverse ways by postmodernity and who in their own way engage with its implications. We both also have elderly living parents. Hence our 'Janus' vision – looking in two different directions.

A case study

We well remember a case study of a young couple in cross-cultural mission who lived, served, birthed and raised their children and saw God alive and well in non-Western contexts. It was almost like living in Acts 29. The significance of this case study is that it was (and is) an intergenerational case study, where an older generation invested in a younger one.

This young couple represented such contrasts. Opposites must attract! She was so young, only twenty-three, when she was plunged, by her husband, already a third-culture person, into another culture. He was all of twenty-eight, but not as mature as she in many ways, and much less aware of himself.

He had come from an evangelical, very low church missionary family and subculture. She was high episcopalian from a very special economic and cultural suburb of the US. It had to have been God that put them together. But above all, she loved God, and had said she was willing to pay any price, go anywhere, do anything, if she was sure God was in it. So she married him.

Both were restless, both were gifted (she as classical musician; he in Spanish, teaching and theology), both were well-trained university graduates. She was possibly too good-looking, too much of an intellectual. One missionary woman belittled her early on with the challenge, 'Why do you have to use such big words?' This was not confidence building for her! She frankly preferred conversation with the men because they grappled with ideas and critical issues. Her classical music training was suspect as not specifically 'Christian' or 'evangelical'.

He thought he was a gracious critic of things as they were, asking the questions that would lead to a new future. He did not always respond in the right way to situations, and there were conflicts with leadership. He assumed his wife would adapt into the missionary subculture. They had entered into a mission subculture that was known to him (he thought it was 'normal') and radically unknown to her (she knew it was not a healthy 'normal').

They were not helped by some of their friends back in their passport culture. His former best friend had 'prophesied' soon after their departure to Latin America that 'They'll be back in six months because she can't cut it.' Well, she lasted seventeen years, and it's a good thing that the Old Testament injunctions against false prophets no longer apply!

Those who knew them understood them as catalysts of change by their lifestyle; by the choices for their children's education; by their commitment to the arts; by their deep friendships with national believers; by applying critical thinking to existing ways of doing things; by initiating new models of ministry; by pondering what it might mean to leave some kind of a legacy; by attempting to leave well and in the right timing. But none of this was easy. There was criticism from the 'missionary establishment', especially (though not exclusively) from the older generation.

It was not an easy seventeen years of cross-cultural mission. But they hung in and persevered in the context of hard lessons. A major crisis arose during their first term when it became evident that irreconcilable differences might lead to an early return to their 'home' country. In the providence of God, the husband in particular was 'saved' by an older mission leader who unexpectedly arrived at their home late one night and sensed the need for healing presence, assurance and prayer.

They never forgot that someone much older than they were had believed in them. Actually, he was the CEO of their mission society, who had taken risks on their behalf, and had encouraged them to think outside the box. This man had spoken prophetically into their lives early on in their field career, saying that their long-term future would not be in that society nor in that ministry. It was an astonishing word, especially for the young husband. But it would in time come to pass.

They stayed until it became clear that it was time to move on to another geographical area and another ministry. God's assignment for them there had been completed. So they left that field – a mutually wrenching experience for them and their Guatemalan friends.

Yet, as a family, they returned many times during the succeeding years to the scenario of that priceless season of life and ministry where their three children were born and raised as trilingual, third-culture persons. They returned to see the gifts of God in the ongoing legacy of those seventeen years and to allow those seminal shapings of their family to continue to be nourished and developed.

We know this case study so very well for it is our story. We are that couple, now much shaped and tempered by our ongoing pilgrimage with God as well as by life, by God's understandings and by global mission. What's more, that mission leader was Bill's own father. He was the key person who believed in us, who saw what our future might be, who encouraged us when Bill, in particular, was about to throw in the towel and return home in shattering personal discouragement and disillusionment.

This mission elder taught us another huge lesson. As CEO of the mission society, at age fifty-nine he announced to the board that he planned to resign the position so that he and mother could return to field ministry, this time in Spain. The board was stunned, and its banker chairman said, 'Bill you can't do this. No bank president returns to be a teller.' My dad replied, 'I don't work in a bank. You people better take me seriously.' And they did. Dad's indelible lesson to me was, 'Bill, leave when they want you to stay, instead of trying to stay when they want you to leave.' How's that for generational grace?

Having ourselves experienced the positives and negatives of generational dynamics we have a special love for and commitment to the younger generations emerging on to the scene of global mission.

Transitioning to a wide-lens template: the Western world transfers

What are these transitions?

They include generations, world views, unfathomed wealth and power. This is evident in politics (think of Reagan to Clinton in the USA; Thatcher to Blair in the UK). They are present in societal structures, whether secular or Christian, and we are certainly witnessing these changes in both church and mission models. Generational issues are different in each nation, though in Western nations (Europe, Australia, New Zealand, North America) there are significant overlaps. How we engage with this transition is crucial, whether we consider ourselves to be in the older or the younger generations. Though I, Bill, have entered my sixth decade, I am very much aware that there are older generations that still control the systems and the power. And I certainly am aware of the younger generations that follow me. So, how must we understand them and engage them as our younger sisters and brothers?

First, we must see them as the first generation shaped by postmodernity. All of us are aware of the massive shift of the Western cultural substrata: we have moved from modernity/secularization into a world increasingly shaped by postmodernity through mass media, the university world, the arts and the forces of economic globalization.

Modernity was characterized by high faith in order, progress, technology and the future, and by rationality and science. Postmodernity is more fluid: there is less faith in order, or progress, or technology, or a hopeful future. It's less rational and less committed philosophically to technology. Yet the younger generations are highly wired. Postmoderns are open to the spiritual, some the serious, but more of them 'dabble in transcendence'. There's an astonishing growth in study programmes on religion and spirituality in the American universities. Yet postmodernity also tends to be committed to an unyielding religious pluralism, an intolerant tolerance that rejects exclusive Truth claims such as that found in Christianity. 'Jesus, Mohammed, the Buddha; Coke, Pepsi, beer – it's just a matter of my personal choice.'

So, when we think of postmodern Christians in global mission, we are thinking of this first generation that has been profoundly shaped by postmodern culture and world view. Naturally, many of them will be deeply critical of modernity and the generations shaped by that world view, in particular the Boomers.

Sadly, the church in the West has generally forgotten or rejected its calling to operate in the realm of open supernaturalism and how to tell creatively our great story to this generation. Additionally, how can we encourage the release of creativity needed by both younger and older generations who want to try new ideas on how we evangelize and disciple, or even how we define and 'do' church and church-in-mission? What will it mean to live out Christianity and mission in and 'not yet of' post-modern culture? Postmodernists owe a debt to history. They also owe to the generation that will follow them, the Millennials, a good and lasting legacy.

Are postmodernists a transitional generation in terms of Christianity and Christian mission? InterVarsity Missions staff member Paula Harris recently wrote us:

> It's interesting, last Urbana (2000) when we had the first group of millennial, our commitment rate doubled as compared to the 80s and 90s when we had Xers at Urbana. I mean twice as many students made missions commitments, made long-term commitments, and were basically excited about our message … 'God wants you to become a missionary and you'll probably suffer for the gospel' (we had a widow testify that night, persecuted church stuff, etc.).

Second, we must see Generation Xers in Christian mission as authentically Christian. As we evaluate these younger genera-tions, especially Generation Xers, consider if you will the verbal dialectic 'on the one hand … on the other hand'.

On the one hand, most of those we know as followers of Jesus are highly committed to Christ. They are highly trained and highly gifted. Many have opted for low-pay vocations with no secular power. Restless, they ask a lot of hard questions. On the other hand, so many of them are unparented, or have been misshaped by the lousy parenting job done by so many Boomers. So many of them come from broken families.

On the one hand, many of them use a new language of meta-physics and epistemology, that is, 'truth' and 'Truth'. Some of them find it hard to use phrases like 'I believe in the absolute truth of (such and such doctrine)'. Yet at the bottom line of their heart and life they are deep believers in the very same thing. So it behoves us to watch their fruit and not just hope to hear our coded phrases we assume we need spoken in order to 'feel comfortable' about them. On the other hand, while many of them are risk takers, some are rather unfocused and even sometimes arrogant in their demeanor. A good number are currently unwilling to submit to existing structures – and that can be both good and bad. Many criticize the older missionary emphasis on longer-term (or even 'career') mission service, and charge that 'longevity alone is no virtue'. They may be right in some ways, but then too many of them appear to be unfocused and they have difficulty sticking to something for more than two years. They seem to want it all. Yet again, on the other hand, we appreciate that they are comfortable in the global village and demonstrate a healthy, holistic perspective on life and mission.

A word to the younger leaders emerging into this scenario of Christian mission

In Spanish there's a lovely phrase '*Les hablo con el corazón en la mano*,' which literally means, 'I speak with my heart in my hand.' It refers to an honest, open-hearted, all-cards-on-the-table speaking the truth in love. So as we speak to the younger generations of leaders whom God has anointed to assume positions of great responsibility and authority in world mission structures, let us speak from the heart.

First, feel free to critique the past – generations, world views, structures. This is needed and is at the core of each responsible generation's contribution to their world. But also be sure to demonstrate your capacity to critique your own generations, their world views, and the structures they propose for the future. It's not easy to speak prophetically to one's own generation, but neither is it impossible.

Second, develop the capacity to stick to something longer than two years. Show you've got the stuff. Reduce bouncing around.

Don't be an expert in short-term commitment. Think of life and job commitments as a series of five-year linkages. Now, we agree that there is no premium nor automatic blessing of God for longevity, *per se*. But there is something about demonstrating the capacity to hang in on an assignment that may not offer all we want; sticking to it for the sake of finishing well a given segment of our lives.

Third, counter the pressures of your own culture by identifying these and their implications on your own life and future. This is your own reading and re-reading of Romans 12:1–2, where you have the ability to discern just where your dominant world view is pressuring you into its mould, which is not that of the Kingdom of God. What are the strengths and weaknesses of postmodernity? How do both these positives and negatives show up in your generation? How does the empowering Spirit of God enable you to become overcomers?

Fourth, learn to accept jobs of low pay, limited recognition and even hardship. A good number of you have spoken with eloquence about holistic ministry and the need for the endowed and rich Western church to demonstrate true compassion and justice for the oppressed and downtrodden of our world and its bruised individuals, families and cultures. So the word for you is to put your money and life where your mouth is.

Fifth, don't devalue pre-field training. We recognize that academic degrees do not guarantee gifted or effective cross-cultural workers or leaders. But we're concerned with the amateurization of mission, or what my anthropologist friend Miriam Adeney calls the 'McDonaldization of mission'. At the same time, we encourage you to value all the various categories of training in equipping for mission. They can be *non-formal* (another word for 'life'), for learning on the job, for purposeful mentoring or even reparenting, for spontaneous lessons of life well appropriated. They can include informal education that speaks of purposeful equipping that takes place outside of the classroom and includes internships, distance education done for personal advancement and not academic certification, or technical on-the-job training. *Formal education* (another term for 'schooling') is for the academy, for designed training and learning done through educational institutions. The best pre-field equipping for cross-cultural ministry is that which combines all modes, where together they shape values, communicate intentional learning and teach skills that are valuable for this God-marketplace of cross-cultural mission.

Sixth, if you come to young adulthood with significant deficits in parenting and mentoring, find those who can meet these needs. Make yourself vulnerable. Seek out the sages, the mothers and the fathers who can value and draw out the God-given and unique giftings that you have. I think these people are best found in the context of the local church, though they also can be tracked down in vocational Christian ministry, whether cross-cultural or not. Ask God to raise up a battalion of mothers and fathers for your broken generation.

Seventh, ask God to allow you to become fully creative risk takers, yet people who are humble and teachable. Ask God to make you ongoing learners. Become passionate followers of the Triune God, rooted in his fatherhood, his Christ and his Spirit. Ask God to help you become people characterized by deep and substantive knowledge of God's Word. Love it, respect it, treasure it, apply it. Mull it over and let it mull you over. Be transformed by it.

Ask God to allow you to be people known as lovers of the family of Christ. This includes his church – universal, global and local. The church is the Body and Bride of Christ, and the Father really loves it. So should you.

Pray that the Father will enable you to become sons and daughters of Issachar, knowing the global times, the historical times, the generational times, the future times. As you discern the needs of your historical moment you will be able to provide the discerning leadership needed to take the church and its mission into the future.

Finally, ask God to make you lovers of intergenerationality. Our experiences in Latin America and in our own church in Austin, Texas, Hope Chapel, have taught us so much in this regard. Since its founding, Hope's leadership has consciously

worked to build and sustain relationships between the generations. It's a joy to see spontaneous and natural cross-relationships
of older with younger, and younger with older. We have observed
courageous love from loving elders who speak truth in love
towards their younger friends.

A word to the older mission leaders of the existing structures

Again, '*Les hablo con el corazón en la mano*' ... 'I speak with my
heart in my hand.' I, Bill, have lived long enough to own a set of
scars that come from ministry: from mistakes; from attempting to
propose and execute things that have not been before; from well-
deserved or perhaps unmerited criticism. I have been a vocal
player in the missions movement. Not everybody agrees with me,
and that's just fine. I don't agree with a number of other people
myself! For some reason God has given us as a married couple the
anointing of mother and of father. That means that as elders we
have experienced a special love for and connection with our
younger friends. Speaking on behalf of our younger colleagues,
we offer the following suggestions as a possible starting point for
bridging the generational gap and opening up space for the
emerging leaders of the future.

First, read this book with loving care. Keep in mind the intention of the writers. Don't get bent out of shape by preconceptions
or by something said that you vigorously disagree with. But do
listen to the intent of the heart that may go beyond the words
written.

Second, check your own gut feeling about the restless younger
women and men with a heart for God who also feel his heart for
the nations. What were you like twenty, thirty, forty or more
years ago? Did you irritate some of your elders, whether in your
family, the church or mission structures? So cut the younger
generation some slack – a lot of slack. Try to imagine what it's like
not to have been parented well, or parented at all. Listen 'between
the lines' for the cry of their woundedness and brokenness. While

you don't excuse them simply for that, it will help you understand and be patient with them.

Third, ask yourself how you are opening up space for them in church and mission structures. This may imply a degree of high risk. Study some of the experience of other colleagues and organizations and what they have done to create space for the younger generations. What lessons can you learn, whether positive or negative?

I, Bill, have been greatly encouraged by a case study in the UK – the story of Stanley Davies and Richard Tiplady of Global Connections (formerly known as the Evangelical Missionary Alliance of the UK). Here we have a tested model of organizational renewal, or space opened up; of responsibility, authority and the opportunity to fail or to succeed given to a younger leader. It's a model to learn from and to follow.

Fourth, evaluate other case studies of organizational transformation, rebranding and generational transfer. These could be from the secular world (and they do exist) or from the Christian world. We're not all that excited about churches that say they cater only for postmoderns, Millennials or whatever. These experiments are destined to fail because they violate the core of the nature of the church of Christ. The church is not intended to be homogenous (though this anthropological model may generate numerical growth). The church is women and men, it's intergenerational, it's multi-ethnic, it embraces people from all socio-economic backgrounds and it challenges all to become new people in the image of Christ.

Fifth, don't place younger leaders into leadership or into token positions just as show cases. We don't need more acolytes in Christian leadership. We need to develop serious internships that open up both responsibility and authority for them.

Sixth, if you are a senior mission leader, it's probably not too late to at least start praying over your succession in leadership. Beware of what's called 'founder's syndrome', where the key genesis leader of an organization is unable to turn it over to a successor. I, Bill, have the example of my father, who, at the age of fifty-nine, left his position as CEO of a mission organization and who with my mother became a field missionary again under the leadership of a much younger man who had joined the mission during Dad's tenure. Leave in the fullness of time rather than hang on. Prepare well and proactively for a timely and healthy handover to younger leaders.

It's important to realize that we can move laterally in Christian ministry and cross-cultural mission leadership even as we transfer leadership to the younger generation. It's not the old myth of 'working myself out of a job', but rather finishing well each segment of God's assignment for us, and moving on into the next assignment.

Seventh, and finally, look to build relationships with two to four younger women and men who are seeking after God. Open space for them, test, encourage, mentor, speak hard and gracious wisdom into their lives. But above all, be vulnerable as you pilgrimage together.

A final word

For a number of years, Yvonne and I have had a deep sense of God's destiny for the upcoming younger generations. God has called us to serve our younger sisters and brothers as a mother and a father. This involves being available to them to invest, to dialogue, to mentor and challenge, to guide and to journey together – all within the context of relationship and love.

There are others within our own generation who feel that same calling and desire. We pray that they will step forward and offer themselves as 'wounded healers' and sages in the service of the emerging generations.

Afterword

<www.postmission.com>

The postmission debate continues ...

Peter Stephenson

The Holy Island Roundtable came about almost by accident. Somehow workers in various missions agencies made contact with each other and began to network informally until Richard Tiplady decided to create an opportunity for younger missions leaders to get together for a few days. For many of us it was a highly significant event because at last we were able to discuss our concerns about the way mission was being done without immediately having our ideas rubbished by those who have a vested interest in keeping things the way they are.

But what of those who were unable to go to Holy Island? What of those who knew nothing of the network that was developing? What of those who are in isolated missions locations, struggling with the kinds of issues we have sought to raise in this book, but doing so totally alone with no one to share ideas, concerns and dreams with? What about those of you reading this book? All of us who were at Holy Island know too many people in these such situations who have given up on mission and sometimes on the church and God as well. We were painfully aware that of the seventeen of us who gathered at Holy Island only a few were actually 'field missionaries' with the rest in communications or leadership roles at head offices. How were we to widen the networking to include those working overseas, where the missionary establishment tends to be even more conservative than at the home end?

The postmission web site <www.postmission.com> is an attempt to widen the network of people committed to discovering what mission should look like for a new generation of Christians in the emerging postmodern global culture. We have posted a number of important articles and papers on the web site to resource those who want to understand better what the issues are. We are developing a section recommending books that are helpful for making sense of the global changes that are taking place and their impact on mission.

Perhaps most importantly of all we have created an Internet forum where anyone, anywhere in the world, can join in an ongoing and wide-ranging discussion of what it means to do authentic Christian mission in an authentically postmodern cultural paradigm. But not only that. We also hope that the forum will create a virtual community where those who feel isolated in their desire to interact meaningfully with postmodernity can find encouragement, support, stimulation and correction – otherwise they would feel totally alone, just like the authors of this book did before God linked them to each other.

Is <www.postmission.com> needed? The responses we had during our first few weeks on line suggest that it is. Here's what people have written to us:

First things first – great site! All the best as you run with this project, it's a great idea and I hope lots of people will jump on board.

At last I have discovered a network of people via your new web site who appear to be on a similar journey to my own!! Anyway, it is with much excitement that I came across your site and network.

Hi. I visited the site. It's good and I'll be back!!!

Much appreciated and helpful. I forwarded the URL to others. Keep up the good work.

Thank you for writing to us about your new web site. We like what you are doing, and intend to promote it and help in whatever ways we can.

Well done for getting things up and running and I wish (not quite the right word!) you all the best for continued growth and effect.

I'm impressed by your site. I must spend more time there – I think there's potential for some useful tie-ups between what you're doing and ourselves.

I looked at your web site. Very good stuff.

Like your idea, concept, web page. I like the thinking behind your site. Will be very interested in your progress and initiative. God bless.

Thank you so much for passing on the info on this site. My best friend and I have been contemplating these ideas for a while now, and often feel like a minority party.

A fellow colleague in my ministry organization introduced me to your web site today. I must say, I was very encouraged by what I discovered. Thanks for pulling your creative and spiritual energy together to co-ordinate this informative and thought-provoking forum. I will forward your web site address on to the senior leadership of our organization, as well as to those within my sphere of influence.

In just the first full month of operation (back in January 2002) the site had over 700 visits. It keeps growing. People have accessed the site from the USA, UK, Spain, Australia, New Zealand, Canada, India, Singapore, Peru, France, South Africa, Brazil, Switzerland, Poland, Mexico, Argentina, Guatemala, The Netherlands, Italy, Belgium, Latvia, Colombia, Denmark, Italy and Japan.

<www.postmission.com> webmaster